THE OFFICIAL

Newcastle United

FANS' GUIDE

THIS IS A CARLTON BOOK

This edition published in 1997

10 9 8 7 6 5 4 3 2 1

A CIP catalogue record for this book is available from the British Library.

ISBN 1 85868 409 9

Project Editor: Martin Corteel
Project art direction: Paul Messam
Production: Garry Lewis and Sarah Schuman
Picture research: Lorna Ainger
Designed by Nigel Davies

Author's acknowledgements
The author would like to thank the staff at Newcastle United Football
Club, the editorial team at *Black and White* magazine and the editors at
Carlton Books for their help and assistance.

Printed in Italy

THE OFFICIAL
Newcastle United

NEWCASTLE UNITED ™

FANS' GUIDE

THE STORY OF
THE PREMIER LEAGUE YEARS

PAUL JOANNOU

CARLTON

Contents

Newcastle and England Number Nine Alan Shearer.

Kenny Dalglish talks things over with his coaches.

The Toon Army at the FA Charity Shield 1996.

Introduction

To the thousands of Newcastle United supporters on Tyneside and around the country, the last five years have been a period to savour. The late Seventies and much of the Eighties were periods of great despondency as the club went through years of struggle both on and off the field. Newcastle failed to compete in the top division with any sort of authority; the club regularly sold their best players before they reached their prime and, as the Nineties opened, United was languishing at the wrong end of the old Division Two.

Meanwhile in the boardroom, there were huge financial problems to rectify. Despite good support at the turnstiles, Newcastle United were heavily in debt. St James' Park needed a total transformation and the club needed millions of pounds to carry it out. Directors and shareholders became locked in a bitter war for control of the club. The famous Magpies were nearly buckling at the knees.

But a saviour was found in the shape of millionaire Sir John Hall, a local entrepreneur who wanted to see the whole North-East region a prosperous and vibrant one. And one of the ways of putting smiles on the faces of the local people was to have a successful football team. Sir John completed his take-over of the club in 1992 and, from that point, Newcastle United have never looked back. Their new owner began a crusade to turn the Magpies into one of the best clubs in all of Europe.

With a Geordie hero in the shape of Kevin Keegan installed as manager, the club rapidly won promotion by lifting the Division One crown in 1993. And the former England skipper made sure his team played the game in a style that pleased everybody. It was football with attacking flair – football that was exciting.

Newcastle joined the FA Premiership as a bright new light and were quickly recognized as a new force in the game. Their brand of stylish football had an immediate impact. Keegan brought in talented and skilful players as Sir John Hall released millions of pounds for transfers. And Newcastle's star-studded line-up very quickly developed into one of the new mega-clubs of the Premiership.

United now competed with the best in the country. They have a redeveloped stadium to be proud of, and a side packed with international players from Britain and around the world. The club's finances have been transformed behind the scenes to a point where they are now one of the biggest and richest operations in the country.

Now another huge personality in the game, Kenny Dalglish, has taken over from Keegan. His challenge is to guide the club from being "The Entertainers" of the Premiership to becoming a trophy-winning side – over and over again, both at home and abroad.

This book charts for supporters Newcastle United's dramatic rise to power in the Premiership. A celebration of the glorious revival of football on Tyneside that has brought smiles to the faces of the Toon Army, it is packed with information on the games played; the players; the personalities; the magnificent St James' Park stadium; as well as the Magpies' full Premiership records up to the end of the 1996–97 season.

The book also gives an insight into the history and traditions of Newcastle United, a club at the very heart of Tyneside life.

Left: Tino's Talk of the Toon. Colombian international Faustino Asprilla is a Premier League superstar.

The History of Newcastle

The origins of Newcastle United Football Club belong to Victorian Tyneside and to two local sides, Newcastle East End and Newcastle West End. Situated on either side of the city, these two pioneering teams developed from humble beginnings as offshoots of cricket clubs during the early 1880s.

A great rivalry existed between the two for a number of years, but by 1892 it was the East Enders who had become the dominant force. West End ran into financial problems and were forced to cease trading. On their demise, East End moved across the city and took over West End's ground, St James' Park. They quickly changed their name to Newcastle United and their red-and-white colours to the now famous black-and-white stripes. Newcastle United were elected to the Football League in 1893 and embarked on an incident-packed century that has made the Magpies one of the game's headliners.

Promotion from the second division was earned rapidly. In 1898, United were elevated to the top division after a series of Test matches – an early version of today's Play-offs. United went on to develop what became Edwardian England's supreme side, but not before the Tynesiders endured a worrying period due to lack of support at the turnstile and lack of money in the bank. But with the help of the directors the club was propped up and survived to become a force in the game.

Household names

Newcastle started to purchase talented players, especially from Scotland, and soon had a squad to rival any in England, featuring such men as Colin Veitch, Jackie Rutherford, Jimmy Lawrence, Albert Shepherd, Bill McCracken, Jimmy Howie, Peter McWilliam and Andy Aitken. All were household names.

Newcastle lifted the League Championship trophy on three occasions and reached five FA Cup finals in the years leading up to the First World War in 1914. Geordie fans enjoyed 10 years of being the team that everyone wanted to topple. The Magpies played an entertaining, rousing style of possession football which became celebrated in the game's history. And they had the stars to go with it too, heroes in much the same mould as today's idols Alan Shearer and Faustino Asprilla.

After the war, the Twenties proved just as eventful. The Magpies lifted the FA Cup at Wembley in 1924, defeating Aston Villa in only the second final to be staged at the famous stadium, and the record signing of Scottish international centre-forward Hughie Gallacher made sure United collected another Championship three years later, in 1927. Famous names continued to pull on the Newcastle striped

NEWCASTLE UNITED AFC 1907-1908.

J.Q. McPHERSON. J.HOWIE. W.McCRACKEN. F.SPEEDIE.   P.McWILLIAM. J.McCLARENCE. R.ORR.   F.G.WATT *secrety*
(TRAINER)
J.W.BELL. J.RUTHERFORD. C.M.VEITCH.   J.CARR.   G.G.ARCHIBALD.   J.GRAHAM
Director   *Director*   *(Director)*
R.W.MACKENZIE.   W. APPLEYARD.   A.GOSNELL.
Director   A.GARDNER. J.BELL. J.P.OLIVER.   S.F.BATES
D.CRAWFORD.   *(vice-chairman) Director)*
Director   *INSET* A.McCOMBIE.   F.G.WATT *(secty)*
J.LUNN. J.CAMERON.
Director *(Chairman)*
G.F.DUFFY.   J.LAWRENCE.   T.S.SINCLAIR.   H.BROWN.   R.OLIVER

MILNE

G. T. Milne   A. McCombie.   R. Oliver
                                                                      Director

Newcastle United at the height of their Edwardian mastery. The Football League trophy (top, middle) and Sheriff of London Charity Shield are shown off in 1907. The Magpies won three titles and appeared in five FA Cup finals during this era before World War One.

shirt: apart from the legendary Gallacher, the Magpies fielded the likes of Neil Harris, Stan Seymour and Frank Hudspeth. Seymour was to become an influential figure over the next 40 years as player, manager and director.

It was back to Wembley in 1932 to compete in the infamous "Over The Line" FA Cup final with Arsenal. United won the game 2–1 after scoring following a cross from Jimmy Richardson which appeared to be hit from out of play – over the line. There were no action replays in those days and the referee allowed the goal – creating a controversial talking-point in FA Cup history.

Newcastle now boasted masters such as Sammy Weaver and Jack Allen, as well as the first player-manager in the top division in Scottish international Andy Cunningham. But after glory beneath the twin towers of Wembley, Newcastle's form slumped and by 1934 they had been relegated for the first time in their history. Amazingly, in the same season as they fell into Division Two, United defeated Liverpool 9–2 and Everton 7–3 in the space of a week!

A rebuilding process took place in the years leading up to the Second World War in 1939. By that time, former star winger Stan Seymour had been appointed to the Board of Directors. Seymour was a strong-willed character, and during the war years he laid the foundations of United's next great period. By the time peace returned, Seymour was at the forefront of affairs, manager in all but name. He ensured the Magpies possessed an entertaining team, full of stars, blending home-grown talent such as Jackie Milburn, Bobby Cowell and Ernie Taylor with big-name signings including George Robledo, Joe Harvey, Bobby Mitchell and Frank Brennan. It was to be a decade of tremendous football as United returned to the limelight.

Hughie Gallacher, who skippered United to the 1927 League title, leads the team out at Highbury.

Hughie GALLACHER

Hughie Gallacher is considered by many to be the greatest centre-forward of all time. Although standing a mere 5ft, 5in tall, the Lanarkshire born star was a quite devastating striker, netting an amazing 463 goals in a career lasting 624 games. Newcastle tracked the Scottish international for several months before signing him for a club record fee of £6,500 in December 1925. And immediately "Wee Hughie" took Tyneside by storm, hitting goals by the score. Gallacher formed a special bond with supporters, especially after skippering Newcastle to the Football League title in 1927. He left United in 1930 after scoring 143 goals in 174 appearances.

Back at the top

Newcastle returned to Division One in double-quick time, achieving promotion in 1948 before vast crowds. Almost 57,000 watched each United home fixture, a record for decades to come. That was just the start of a period of success that saw the FA Cup return to St James' Park three times; in 1951, 1952 and 1955. United were known in every corner of the country, and so were their players; "Wor Jackie" and "Bobby Dazzler" were the pick of a side renowned across the nation.

Despite fielding quality players throughout the Fifties – men such as Ivor Allchurch, George Eastham and Len White – United slipped from Division One in 1961 under the controversial managership of ex-Manchester United player Charlie Mitten. But an old war-horse returned in the shape of Joe Harvey. He had skippered the Magpies to many of their early Fifties successes, and now teamed up with Seymour to revitalize the club as Newcastle returned to the ranks of the élite as Division Two champions in 1965.

Into Europe – and out again

Football's modern era has seen United as an unpredictable side, always capable of defeating the best but, until recently, never quite realizing their huge potential. Joe Harvey's side qualified for Europe for the first time in 1968 and stunned everyone the following year by lifting the Inter-Cities Fairs Cup, the forerunner of the UEFA Cup. That has been Newcastle's only European trophy to date.

Since their earliest years, Newcastle have traditionally fielded a famous Number Nine at centre-forward, and this was to continue, with big Welshman Wyn Davies prominent along with the likes of striker Bryan "Pop" Robson and defenders Bobby Moncur and Frank Clark. United had a solid team rather than a flamboyant one, but in the years which followed that European success, manager Harvey brought in a string of talented entertainers who thrilled the Gallowgate crowd, including pleasers such as Jimmy Smith, Tony Green and Terry Hibbitt and especially a new centre-forward – named Malcolm Macdonald.

Nicknamed "Supermac", Malcolm Macdonald was one of United's biggest hero figures. Brash, arrogant and devastating in front of goal, he led United's attack to Wembley twice, in 1974 and 1976, against Liverpool in the FA Cup and Manchester City in the League

United line-up in the early Fifties: Back row (l to r): Cowell, Stokoe, Fairbrother, Corbett, Hannah, Crowe; Front: Walker, Robledo, Brennan, Milburn, Mitchell.

Cup. On each occasion, however, the Magpies failed to bring the trophy back to Tyneside.

On the slide

As the Eighties got under way, United slumped. Macdonald had gone to Arsenal and the Geordies were languishing in Division Two. Gordon Lee had replaced Joe Harvey as boss, yet he in turn soon gave way to Richard Dinnis and then Bill McGarry. But it was Arthur Cox who steered United back to Division One again, with a little help from a certain Kevin Keegan who joined Newcastle in a sensational deal in 1982. The England captain transformed Cox's promotion plans. Keegan captivated everyone on Tyneside and United stormed into the top division in a style only bettered by Kevin's own brand of football in the next decade. Alongside Keegan were bright youngsters Peter Beardsley and Chris Waddle, as well as seasoned campaigners such as Terry McDermott – a 1974 FA Cup finalist with United – and David McCreery.

Paul Gascoigne soon followed, as did Jack Charlton as manager. Newcastle consolidated their place in Division One, but then a period of selling their best players – Beardsley, Waddle and Gazza – rocked the club, as did a share war for control of Newcastle United. The Magpies tumbled back into Division Two and were in a perilous state: they had little money, their star players were heading south and crowds were dwindling. Newcastle United needed a saviour. They not only got one but two, in the shape of Sir John Hall and Kevin Keegan.

Jackie MILBURN

Universally known as "Wor Jackie" and a legend in the North East, Jackie Milburn was recognized as one of the best centre-forwards during the glorious Fifties era. Blessed with killing pace, a lethal shot, as well as charm and modesty, Milburn became an immense idol on Tyneside – which continued long after he stopped playing. Jackie still holds the club scoring record – 239 goals in 494 appearances from 1943 to 1957 – many of which were spectacular strikes. He came from a famous footballing family that also produced Bobby and Jack Charlton.

Supermac – Malcolm Macdonald became a star following his record transfer from Luton in 1971.

Malcolm MACDONALD

Malcolm Macdonald was known throughout the land as "Supermac". Strong and powerful, he wore the Number Nine shirt at St James' Park with the aim of scoring as many goals as possible. He lived for hitting the back of the net and in a style that meant excitement, crashing goals from all distances and angles – once from the halfway line. Costing United a £180,000 fee from Luton Town in 1971, Supermac was the hero of Tyneside before moving to Arsenal in 1976. In 258 games for United he scored 138 goals. He also scored five goals in an England match.

Newcastle's biggest modern hero, the charismatic Kevin Keegan who first arrived on Tyneside in 1982.

Kevin KEEGAN

When Kevin Keegan first joined United from Southampton in August 1982 for £100,000, the whole of Tyneside was buzzing with Keegan-mania – Mark I. Scoring on his debut against Queens Park Rangers, the former Liverpool and England captain guided the Magpies back to Division One in 1983–84. His experience and skill were the keys to Newcastle's line-up getting together in a way that brought entertaining, skilful and attacking football back to Tyneside for two years. He top-scored with 27 goals as United reached Division One and had much to do with emergence of Peter Beardsley and Chris Waddle as international stars. After retiring as a player in 1984, Keegan returned to United, as boss in 1992 – and Keegan-mania Mark II erupted.

The right man for the job

When Kevin Keegan returned to Tyneside in February 1992, to succeed Ossie Ardiles as manager on a short-term contract, United were struggling at the wrong end of Division Two. Sir John Hall had all but taken control of the club and he needed a small miracle to stop the Magpies from tumbling into Division Three for the first time in their history. If Sir John was to transform the near-bankrupt club, they simply had to survive. Kevin Keegan's job was straightforward. Newcastle could not afford to be relegated: he had to keep the Black-and-Whites up.

Just as before, Keegan's mere presence captivated the region. United's disgruntled supporters became excited, expectant ones overnight. They packed St James' Park again, and at first Newcastle's side was carried up the table on a wave of charged passion. But then a bad run left the Magpies in trouble as the season's crucial stage arrived. An important victory over Portsmouth was achieved: then came the crunch in the final fixture of the season, against Leicerster City, at Filbert Street. United had to win to stay in Division Two. They did so thanks to an own-goal, to joyous relief from the thousands who had made the trip to the Midlands. Keegan had completed his job.

Looking to the future

Sir John Hall now turned his attention to a master-plan to develop Newcastle United into a superclub, not only in England, but in the whole of Europe. He first needed to persuade Kevin Keegan to stay on as manager. During the summer of 1992 the former England star agreed to remain on Tyneside, and immediately the powerful duo swung into action. Sir John began to transform the club's finances and to redevelop St James' Park into a stadium as good as any in Britain. Keegan brought in new players such as Paul Bracewell, Barry Venison and John Beresford. It was the start of five very special years under Keegan's guidance.

Newcastle got off to a winning start in the 1992–93 season: in fact they could not stop winning, going on a run of 11 victories in a row. Keegan's new side was top of the table and the talk of the land. His brand of exciting and flamboyant football delighted the country, and United rapidly became a national favourite.

Newcastle kept their lead at the top of the division for most of the season, making them dead certs to gain promotion to the new Premier League – and with it huge financial benefits. New faces began to arrive who would serve the club well in the seasons to come: Robert Lee was picked up from Charlton, Scott Sellars arrived from Leeds and Keegan smashed United's transfer fee record when he paid £1.75 million for Andy Cole, a young and somewhat untried striker from Bristol City.

Keegan's judgement proved first-class, however, as Cole took over the Number Nine shirt at St James' Park. Within a few months he was spoken of in the same breath as former United greats such as Gallacher, Milburn and Macdonald. Newcastle's brand of quick-passing possession football was too good for Division One, and as the promotion run-in arrived in the spring, United were ready to bounce into the Premier League as clear champions.

A new era for Newcastle

A single goal from Sellars clinched an important derby victory over Sunderland, then United had a Tuesday-evening fixture with Grimsby at Blundell Park. If they took another three points no one could catch them. A Geordie invasion engulfed Cleethorpes as United went for both promotion and the title.

A goalless first-half was satisfying enough in a tense match, and soon after the restart Robert Lee pushed forward and carried the ball through several Grimsby tackles before releasing Andy Cole in on goal. Cole fired the ball low into the net and Newcastle were on their way. David Kelly added a second near the final whistle and the Tyneside masses burst into raptures. Newcastle were in the Premier League and the first stage in the resurgence of Newcastle United was complete.

The Toon Army celebrated all week, yet no one could have expected the events that took place in the finale to the season against Leicester at St James' Park. Coincidentally, City had been Newcastle's opponents a year before, when United won to escape relegation.

Now the Foxes were in for a roasting as Keegan's dream football was broadcast to the country. United were 6–0 up at half-time and won 7–1! David Kelly grabbed a stunning first-half hat-trick as Newcastle's flowing football ripped the visitors apart. Andy Cole also completed a memorable hat-trick on a memorable day when the League Championship trophy was presented to the Magpies. A warning had gone out to every Premier League club: Newcastle United were back, and back with a bang!

The first sign of United's big spending power was the £1.75m record purchase of Andy Cole during 1993. He immediately made a huge impact.

The Premiership Years

Since the Premier League began in 1993, football in England has never looked back. Newcastle's revival came at the same time and the Magpies have rapidly become one of the Premiership's top guns.

Newcastle United joined the élite of the Premier League for the start of the 1993–94 season. After winning the First Division – and, technically, the Football League – championship, there was frantic activity over the summer to make sure the Magpies were ready for their first taste of the FA Carling Premiership. On the field, Kevin Keegan reinforced his squad, and elsewhere Sir John Hall made sure the redevelopment of St James' Park went ahead at speed. The Leazes End – traditional home of Newcastle's choir – was ready for the start and the revamped arena looked a picture, the equal of any ground in the country.

The Black-and-Whites took only a matter of weeks to establish themselves in the top half of the table and during the first part of the 1993–94 programme they soon became recognized as a new force. Then they quickly climbed even higher, and have rarely been out of the top four in the division since. Only Manchester United can boast a better record than Newcastle's two runners-up spots, a third and a sixth place over their four-year Premiership history.

Newcastle are one of the Premiership's biggest spenders, paying £7.5m for Tino Asprilla (above) and a world record £15m for Alan Shearer (right).

Premiership Record

Season	P	W	D	L	F	A	Pts	Pos.
1993–94	42	23	8	11	82	41	77	3rd
1994–95	42	20	12	10	67	47	72	6th
1995–96	38	24	6	8	66	37	78	2nd
1996–97	38	19	11	8	73	40	68	2nd

Premiership Big Spending

Player	Fee	Previous club
Peter Beardsley	£1.5 million	Everton
Ruel Fox	£2.25 million	Norwich City
Darren Peacock	£2.70 million	QPR
Philippe Albert	£2.65 million	Anderlecht
Paul Kitson	£2.25 million	Derby County
Warren Barton	£4 million	Wimbledon
Les Ferdinand	£6 million	QPR
David Ginola	£2.50 million	Paris St-Germain
Tino Asprilla	£7.50 million	Parma
David Batty	£3.50 million	Blackburn Rovers
Alan Shearer	£15 million	Blackburn Rovers
Jon Tomasson	£2.25 million	Heerenveen
Alessandro Pistoni	£4.30 million	Internazionale Milan

The club has invested heavily in gaining this position. Many millions of pounds have been released by United's directors to enable firstly Keegan, then Kenny Dalglish to attract the very best players to Tyneside. United's squad has been transformed since the dark days of Division Two. The first-team pool has been virtually an all-international one, containing players from throughout Europe and even South America.

But it has not all been big-money purchases. Over this short period at the top, Newcastle's managers have been very businesslike. They may have spent heavily, but it has generally been wisely. And when players have been sold – characters such as Ruel Fox or Andy Cole – it has been for substantial profits. Local products have been utilized, too. Steve Watson has become a regular; so did Robbie Elliott before his move to Bolton, and Lee Clark before going to Sunderland's new Stadium of Light.

That's entertainment!

Throughout Newcastle's development as Manchester United's most persistent challengers for the championship, along with Liverpool, the Tynesiders have built up a reputation for an attacking brand of soccer and been dubbed "The Entertainers". With a total of 288 goals scored against 165 conceded, spectators have witnessed an average of nearly three goals a game. In football terms that's not bad going: as they say, "pure entertainment".

Now, under the guidance of Kenny Dalglish, Newcastle need to build on the foundations laid by Kevin Keegan and secure the Premiership title from the Old Trafford sideboard.

Premiership Full Internationals

Pavel Srnicek, Czech Republic	**Marc Hottiger**, Switzerland
Barry Venison, England	**Les Ferdinand**, England
Steve Howey, England	**Warren Barton**, England
Robert Lee, England	**Keith Gillespie**, Northern Ireland
Peter Beardsley, England	**David Ginola**, France
Tommy Wright, Northern Ireland	**Tino Asprilla**, Colombia
Liam O'Brien, Republic of Ireland	**David Batty**, England
Nicky Papavasiliou, Cyprus	**Alan Shearer**, England
Alan Neilson, Wales	**Shay Given**, Republic of Ireland
Malcolm Allen, Wales	**Temur Ketsbaia**, Georgia
Philippe Albert, Belgium	**Jon Tomasson**, Denmark
	Bjarni Gudjonsson, Iceland

Milestones 1993–94

1 August Transfer activity as Gavin Peacock and David Kelly depart for Chelsea and Wolves, respectively, while Mike Hooper, Niki Papavasiliou and Peter Beardsley arrive at St James' Park. The return of Beardsley for £1.5 million from Everton is a deal to capture the Tyneside public's imagination.

9 August Agony for Beardsley as he is felled by Liverpool's Neil Ruddock in a friendly at Anfield. United's returning hero is out of action for several weeks with a broken jaw.

14 August Newcastle open life in the Premiership with a 1–0 home defeat against Tottenham Hotspur, managed by ex-United boss Ossie Ardiles. A goal by Teddy Sheringham silences the crowd

21 August (17th) The Magpies gain their first point in the Premier League, earning a 1–1 draw against Manchester United at Old Trafford. Ryan Giggs cracks home a free kick to put the Reds 1–0 up, but Andy Cole steals a point when he plants the ball in the net after a neat move.

13 September (13th) A rip-roaring tussle with Sheffield Wednesday takes place at St James' Park. New signings Malcolm Allen and Alex Mathie both find the scoresheet as United take care of the Owls, 4–2, after being 2–1 behind.

25 September (11th) Peter Beardsley returns to the St James' Park turf against West Ham United and marks his comeback by linking up with Andy Cole as the Magpies start to pick up points. The Hammers go down 2–0 and Cole fires home twice.

5 October (11th) Newcastle cruise through in the opening tie of the League Cup campaign. They thrash Notts County 11–2 on aggregate and score seven in the away leg!

24 October (11th) Controversial events as Lee Clark has a row with manager Kevin Keegan – live on television – during the defeat at Southampton. A dispute with Andy Cole follows, but matters are thankfully patched up quickly.

30 October (9th) Wimbledon are thrashed on Tyneside thanks to some inspired play from Peter Beardsley, who completes a brilliant hat-trick. The

Newcastle gained their first point in the Premiership thanks to Andy Cole's strike at Old Trafford.

Magpies are starting to make people sit up and take notice of their quality.

8 November (9th) Following their Sky-televised 3–1 victory at Oldham, Kevin Keegan's line-up more than justify the tag of "The Entertainers". Newcastle are fast becoming one of the headline-makers of the Premiership.

21 November (8th) A fabulous 3–0 victory over Liverpool at St James' Park shows that United have found their feet in the top division. Andy Cole grabs a hat-trick as Newcastle's attack destroys the Reds.

24 November (4th) United make it four wins in a row and climb to fourth place in the table following a 4–0 victory over Sheffield United. Newcastle join Blackburn as one of Manchester United's closest challengers for the title.

11 December (5th) A Robert Lee run and cross, converted by Andy Cole, earns another point against Manchester United in a top-of-the-table clash.

9 February (4th) The Magpies crash out of the FA Cup to Luton Town in a replay at Kenilworth Road. United had missed their chance at St James' Park when they could only claim a 1–1 draw. Two breakaway goals, one in each half, were enough to give the Hatters the chance to travel to Cardiff in the fifth round.

23 February (3rd) Following two Premiership defeats by Wimbledon and Blackburn, Newcastle get back to winning ways with an emphatic 4–0 success over Coventry City on Tyneside. Centre-forward Andy Cole continues his devastating goalscoring burst – he nets a hat-trick.

12 March (3rd) More goals as Swindon Town are rocked with a seven-goal blitz by the Magpies – and this time top scorer Andy Cole doesn't make it on to the scoresheet.

29 March (3rd) Kevin Keegan's big-money dealing begins to create news as Darren Peacock joins the Magpies for a club record of £2.7 million, shortly after Ruel Fox's arrival for £2.25 million. Both assist in United's 3–0 win over Norwich City, the Magpies' fifth win out of five played during March.

16 April (3rd) Newcastle's campaign to secure a European place is given a boost with an excellent 2–0 win over Liverpool at Anfield. Classic goals from Andy Cole and Robert Lee make a big impression on the Premier League.

Peter Beardsley's return to Tyneside was a key factor in United's resurgence in the Premiership.

27 April (3rd) The 40th goal of the season by Andy Cole in a 5–1 thrashing of Aston Villa sets a new club record. Cole topples the long-standing mark held by Hughie Gallacher and George Robledo. And United's five goals ensure they will finish the season with a record haul of goals for the Premiership.

7 May (3rd) United's 2–0 victory over Arsenal at St James' Park means they end their first season in the Premiership in a more than creditable third place, behind Blackburn Rovers and champions Manchester United. The Magpies qualify for the UEFA Cup for the first time since 1977.

Milestones 1994–95

21 August Two new signings, 1994 World Cup stars Philippe Albert and Marc Hottiger, make victorious debuts at Leicester on the opening day of the season. Newcastle secure the points with an impressive 3–1 win. However, there is bad luck for Peter Beardsley: he breaks his jaw for the second year running.

10 September (1st) United's fine start to the season continues with a 4–2 success over Chelsea at St James' Park, with Andy Cole firing home a rocket shot. "Cole for England!" is the cry.

24 September (1st) The Magpies reinforce their position at the top of the Premiership with a six-match winning sequence from the opening fixture – and score 22 goals in the process. A 1–1 draw with Liverpool at St James' Park is the first point dropped.

Kevin Keegan dropped a bombshell when he sold Andy Cole to Manchester United in January 1995.

27 September (1st) The Black-and-Whites establish a 10–2 aggregate victory over Royal Antwerp in the UEFA Cup to set warning bells ringing across Europe. Rob Lee nets four goals in the tie, including a hat-trick in the first leg.

5 October (1st) Newcastle take care of Barnsley in the Coca-Cola Cup thanks to a scoreline of 3–1 over two legs.

18 October (1st) Spanish club Athletic Bilbao face United at St James' Park in the UEFA Cup and find themselves in for a roasting as the Magpies storm to a 3–0 advantage. But, crucially, United give away two late goals to the visitors.

22 October (1st) United keep on track in the Premiership by taking the points in a 2–1 victory over Sheffield Wednesday on Tyneside.

26 October (1st) It is Manchester United's turn to fall to the unstoppable Magpies, losing 2–0 in a Coca-Cola Cup meeting at St James' Park.

29 October (1st) At Old Trafford the Reds gain revenge and put an end to Newcastle's 17-game unbeaten run. Manchester United win the Premiership clash 2–0, but United still head the table.

1 November (1st) Newcastle fall to Athletic Bilbao in the return leg of the UEFA Cup meeting, and after its bright opening Newcastle's season begins to fall apart. Injuries to key players start to ravage Kevin Keegan's squad, with Beardsley, Venison, Sellars, Albert and Cole all out for long periods.

3 December (3rd) Tottenham slam four goals past United at White Hart Lane: the Magpies have not won a Premier League game in four matches.

21 December (3rd) Now United exit the Coca-Cola (League) Cup. Fielding a patched-up side against Manchester City at St James' Park, they lose 2–0 after doing the hard work earning a replay with a draw at Maine Road.

31 December (4th) The year closes with United struggling to find consistent form. They fall 2–1 at Norwich and drop out of the top three for the first time in the season.

10 January (5th) Sensational news as Andy Cole is sold to Manchester United for a record £7 million, with young Keith Gillespie ending up at St James' Park as part of the deal.

15 January (5th) United and Manchester United continue their rivalry with a hard-fought clash at St James' Park which ends 1–1. Paul Kitson earns the Magpies a point.

18 January (5th) Newcastle take part in a great FA Cup replay against Blackburn. At Ewood Park, goals from Marc Hottiger – with a swerving free kick – and Lee Clark give United a fourth-round place.

25 January (4th) Newcastle start to recover league form with a battling 2–1 victory over Wimbledon. Kitson scores another as a temporary replacement for departed star centre-forward Andy Cole.

11 February (3rd) Following a 2–1 success over Nottingham Forest, the Magpies climb back into the top three.

19 February (3rd) After toppling Swansea City in the FA Cup fourth round, Newcastle face their League Cup conquerors Manchester City for a place in the FA Cup quarter-final. Newcastle win 3–1 after a commanding performance.

25 February (3rd) The Magpies' Premiership form continues to improve as Newcastle take care of Aston Villa 3–1; their sixth home victory in a row. Ipswich are soon defeated at Portman Road to put Newcastle back in contention for a European place.

12 March (3rd) The Wembley run comes to an end as Everton knock United out of the FA Cup in the sixth round at Goodison Park: a 65th-minute winner from Dave Watson ends the Toon Army's cup dreams.

14 April (4th) A return to Goodison Park in the Premier League leaves United high and dry after a 2–0 defeat. Newcastle drop to fourth position and are losing ground in the race for a UEFA Cup place.

17 April (5th) A costly home reverse against Leeds United nearly spells disaster for Newcastle's ambitions. A scrappy display means the Magpies have to turn on the style to achieve that European place.

Paul Kitson replaced Andy Cole and did a good until the arrival of Les Ferdinand in the summer.

3 May (5th) A marvellous 3–3 draw with Tottenham Hotspur takes place on Tyneside which thrills the crowd. Two players are sent off – including United's goalkeeper Pavel Srnicek – but crucially United pick up only one point and not three.

8 May (5th) United need all three points as they visit Blackburn Rovers, who in touching distance of the Championship. Newcastle outplay the champions-elect, but return pointless as Alan Shearer claims a vital goal for the Ewood Park club.

14 May (6th) With only an outside chance of gaining a UEFA Cup place, United defeat Crystal Palace 3–2, but results elsewhere end the club's season on a sour note. The Magpies just miss out on another European venture and end in a disappointing sixth place.

Milestones 1995–96

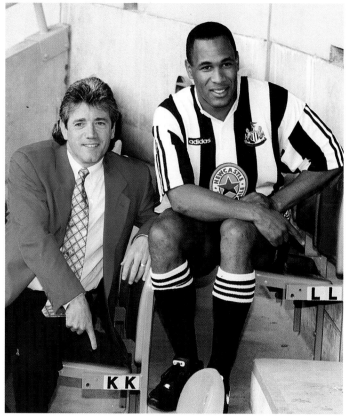

At last Kevin's got his man! After a long chase, Les Ferdinand signs for Newcastle for £6m.

1 August Kevin Keegan's spending spree sends Tyneside wild as Les Ferdinand, Warren Barton, Shaka Hislop and David Ginola arrive at Newcastle for a combined total of more than £14 million.

19 August Newcastle take care of Coventry City in style with a 3–0 win. Les Ferdinand nets on his debut as he takes over the Number Nine shirt.

30 August (1st) Ferdinand is again on the mark against Middlesbrough in the Tyne–Tees derby clash. Newcastle make it four wins out of four played and are at the top of the Premiership again.

16 September (1st) A 3–1 victory over Manchester City at St James' Park keeps United's excellent start going. Ferdinand is on fire and grabs another two goals – six in six games for the £6 million man.

24 September (1st) Ferdinand cannot stop scoring. Another brace find the net and Chelsea are felled 2–0 as Newcastle turn on the entertainment.

4 October (1st) Bristol City are thrashed 8–1 on aggregate in the Coca-Cola Cup. United's display is such that they simply toy with the opposition.

21 October (1st) No one can stop Les Ferdinand as he strikes a hat-trick. Wimbledon are given the hammer and lose 6–1 on Tyneside. United's devastating attack – Ginola and Gillespie on the flanks, Ferdinand and Beardsley in the middle – is celebrated the nation over.

25 October (1st) The goals continue to flow as Stoke City go down 4–0 in the Coca-Cola Cup.

4 November (1st) A tougher game follows for United as they entertain Liverpool at St James' Park. A late winner by Steve Watson settles a marvellous open contest 2–1 to the Black-and-Whites.

8 November (1st) United's big November test is passed as champions Blackburn are beaten 1–0 at St James' Park. Newcastle are clear at the top of the Premiership, eight points ahead of Manchester United.

29 November (1st) Newcastle have a famous victory at Anfield in the Coca-Cola Cup. An absorbing tussle is settled thanks to a marvellous piece of skill by Steve Watson, who strikes a wonder goal to take the tie 1–0.

3 December (1st) More entertainment follows as United and Wimbledon play out a 3–3 spectacle at Selhurst Park. However, Newcastle allow the points to slip away when the match is within their grasp.

23 December (1st) Frenchman David Ginola is on top form as Nottingham Forest are beaten 3–1 in a Christmas meeting on Tyneside. Robert Lee fires in a beauty from 25 yards and Newcastle remain clear favourites to lift the title.

27 December (1st) The first battle of the season between United and the Reds from Old Trafford goes Manchester's way as Andy Cole helps to send a warning to the Black-and-Whites. Newcastle lose 2–0.

10 January (1st) Newcastle fall 2–0 to Arsenal in the League Cup at Highbury. In a controversial match David Ginola clashes with Lee Dixon and is sent off.

17 January (1st) Having been a good bet for a Wembley appearance in either the League Cup or FA

Cup, United find themselves out of both competitions following a disastrous January. They lose to Chelsea following a penalty shoot-out.

20 January (1st) The Magpies keep their grip on the top place in the Premiership with a 2–1 win over Bolton Wanderers at St James' Park.

8 February (1st) Kevin Keegan digs deep once more, paying £7.5 million to bring Colombian international Faustino Asprilla to Newcastle from Italian club Parma and £3.5 million for Blackburn's England midfielder David Batty.

10 February (1st) Tino arrives from the bench in the derby match with Middlesbrough and makes a crucial equalizing goal for Steve Watson. It sets United on their way to a 2–1 victory.

4 March (1st) The championship showdown occurs at St James' Park and Manchester United steal a 1–0 victory despite Newcastle outplaying their rivals for most of the match. It is a crucial set-back.

23 March (2nd) United lose another vital fixture, this time 2–0 at Highbury against Arsenal, and the Magpies' title challenge starts to disintegrate. Manchester United, meanwhile, are getting stronger and stronger, and take the top spot for the first time this season.

3 April (2nd) A classic match at Anfield results in a seven-goal thriller and victory for Liverpool through a last-minute winner by Stan Collymore. United go 2–1 and 3–2 ahead, but still manage to lose 4–3!

8 April (2nd) Newcastle throw away what seems to be a well-earned three points at Ewood Park. After going ahead through a great David Batty strike, United let in two late goals to Blackburn's Wallsend-born striker Graham Fenton and commit suicide in the title race.

29 April (2nd) Entering the title run-in, United's third single-goal victory in a row – over Villa, Southampton and Leeds – keeps them in the race, neck-and-neck with Manchester United.

2 May (2nd) A heartbreaking finale to a terrific championship race as Newcastle again fail to convert a goal advantage into victory, against Nottingham Forest at the City Ground. Peter Beardsley's gem is cancelled out by another late equalizer – and with it goes any chance of lifting the Premiership trophy.

5 May (2nd) Tottenham Hotspur arrive on Tyneside for the final match of the season and United's downcast fans see the title go to Old Trafford as Manchester United win at Middlesbrough. United can only manage to draw 1–1 with Spurs and finish the season in the runners-up spot.

David Batty fires the ball into the Blackburn net to give Newcastle the lead in a crucial fixture on 8 April. However, the Magpies conceded two late goals, to a Geordie-born striker Graham Fenton. The 2–1 defeat cost them three vital points in the race for the FA Carling Premiership crown. The title ended up at Old Trafford again.

Milestones 1996–97

"Shearer's coming home," was the chant after his world-record £15m transfer from Blackburn.

1 August Alan Shearer signs for Newcastle in a spectacular, world-record £15 million deal that stuns the football world.

11 August United crash in the Charity Shield at Wembley, losing 4–0 in the face of a powerful Manchester United display.

17 August (17th) Newcastle start their challenge for the Premiership crown at Goodison Park and fall to Everton 2–0. United's expensive side is given a roasting by the media.

21 August (12th) The Magpies gain their first points of the season with a 2–0 victory over Wimbledon and £15 million signing Alan Shearer grabs his first goal for United.

4 September (8th) In the derby match at Roker Park, Sunderland take the lead, only for United to fight back through goals from Ferdinand and Beardsley.

10 September (6th) Newcastle take a 4–0 first-leg advantage in the UEFA Cup opening round against Swedish part-timers Halmstads. The Magpies eventually go through 5–2 on aggregate.

30 September (2nd) Newcastle climb the Premier League table after a poor opening, and three points in a tremendous match against Aston Villa reinforce their challenge at the top of the division. United win the clash 4–3 against a 10-man Villa team.

12 October (1st) Newcastle go back to the top of the Premiership table thanks a single goal from Alan Shearer in the meeting with Derby County at the Baseball Ground.

20 October (1st) United thrash their rivals Manchester United 5–0, and in great style, to gain revenge for their Wembley drubbing. The Magpies are favourites for the title again.

29 October (2nd) With Hungarians Ferencvaros on Tyneside for the UEFA Cup meeting the Geordies again put on a five-star display, hitting the Continental visitors with four goals to win the tie 6–3 on aggregate.

3 November (1st) After losing the Premier League leadership, a 3–1 victory over Middlesbrough at St James' Park puts the Magpies back on top. Peter Beardsley scores twice to inspire his side to success.

27 November (1st) United crash out of the Coca-Cola Cup after a 3–1 derby reverse at Middlesbrough.

30 November (3rd) With only 10 men, Arsenal inflict a 2–1 home defeat on the Magpies and Newcastle drop to third place in the table.

3 December (3rd) Newcastle take care of French club Metz in the UEFA Cup, winning 2–0 at St James' Park and 3–1 on aggregate.

17 December (4th) A dip in United's form as they lose embarrassingly to relegation strugglers Coventry City. The bookmakers no longer have the troubled Magpies as favourites for the title.

23 December (6th) Newcastle slip to sixth place after a 1–1 draw with fellow title challengers Liverpool. Shearer and Fowler share the spoils with a goal each in an entertaining contest of the highest quality.

26 December (6th) A desperate performance at Blackburn earns the Magpies no points and a roasting from manager Kevin Keegan, who is far from being a happy boss.

28 December (5th) The players respond to criticism and overwhelm Spurs 7–1 at St James' Park. Ferdinand, Shearer and Lee all hit two goals apiece.

5 January (4th) Newcastle travel to The Valley to face Charlton Athletic in the FA Cup third round. The Magpies take the lead through ex-Charlton star Rob Lee, but Athletic equalize and earn a replay. Speculation mounts over the future of Kevin Keegan.

8 January (4th) Kevin Keegan resigns as manager of Newcastle United. Tyneside is in a state of shock at the news, which makes headlines nationwide.

The pressure mounts for Kevin Keegan – Special K is about to call it a day.

14 January (4th) Newcastle's board of directors moves swiftly to appoint a replacement. Kenny Dalglish steps into Keegan's shoes – just like he had done as a player at Liverpool – to appease supporters.

15 January (4th) Newcastle battle through to the next round of the FA Cup and Dalglish gets off to a winning start thanks to a late Alan Shearer free kick in extra time against Charlton.

18 January (4th) Kenny Dalglish comes up against United's old problem of conceding late goals in a 2–2 draw at Southampton. United are 2–0 up but lose their grip on the match in the dying minutes.

26 January (4th) In a fourth-round FA Cup meeting with Nottingham Forest – the Premier League's strugglers – United take the lead, but Forest win 2–1 after Ian Woan fires in a tremendous volleyed winner.

2 February (4th) An Alan Shearer hat-trick against Leicester City dramatically turns a 3–1 deficit into a 4–3 victory, in a match which will live in the memory for years to come.

10 March (4th) Another epic takes place at Anfield, but for the second year running Newcastle fall to Liverpool by a 4–3 scoreline, and to a last-minute winner too!

15 March (4th) Kenny Dalglish's influence gives United a boost in their search for a European place as Coventry City are beaten 4–0 on Tyneside.

18 March (4th) Newcastle are hit by injury as both Shearer and Ferdinand miss the important return leg of the UEFA Cup quarter-final meeting with Monaco. Newcastle have little hope and are soundly defeated 3–0 in France and 4–0 on aggregate.

2 April (4th) News off the field, as the club is at long last floated on the Stock Exchange as a public limited company (plc).

5 April (4th) Newcastle need points to re-establish a title challenge, but can only draw in the Sunderland derby tussle on Tyneside. Shearer and Ferdinand return from injury lay-offs and the England captain earns United a point with a late equalizer.

16 April (4th) Tino Asprilla continues on good form, inspiring United to a 3–1 victory over FA Cup finalists Chelsea at St James' Park. The Colombian's influence is too much for the Londoners.

3 May (4th) In a top-of-the-table meeting at Highbury, Newcastle steal three points from Arsenal and mount a late championship run with Liverpool in the chase to catch Manchester United.

6 May (4th) With games in hand, Newcastle are the only club that can catch Alex Ferguson's men. But the 0–0 draw at Upton Park with West Ham is not enough and the title goes to Old Trafford once more.

11 May (2nd) On a dramatic final day of the season United are in top gear and too much for relegated Nottingham Forest. The Magpies win 5–0 and Arsenal and Liverpool's results mean Newcastle have done just enough to pinch the runners-up spot and claim a place in the European Champions' League.

Chapter 3
Newcastle in Europe

European glory came Newcastle's way in 1969, when they won the Inter-Cities Fairs Cup. Since then a repeat has proved elusive, but in 1997, United make their first foray into the Champions Cup.

Although Newcastle United arrived on the European scene relatively late, in the 1968–69 season, they made an immediate impact by winning a trophy! When the club played its first game in Europe, back in September 1968, jetting the airways of the Continent was something completely new for the whole of the North-East region. And how the public enjoyed it. Thrill and incident followed month after month, and packed houses witnessed three years of gripping fixtures in the Inter-Cities Fairs Cup, the forerunner of the modern UEFA Cup. Today, the Geordie public regards any contest in European competition as something special.

Newcastle have a more than respectable record in European soccer, playing more than 40 games and only losing a handful. And at St James' Park they have been defeated only twice. The European love affair started on an autumn evening in 1968 when Dutch giants Feyenoord arrived on Tynside boasting a fine European pedigree. However, the Magpies showed in no uncertain terms that, although they were European newcomers, they weren't going to be pushovers, and

Wyn Davies – "the Mighty Wyn" to United fans – was a key factor in Newcastle's European success.

Bryan "Pop" Robson, the partner of Wyn Davies in attack as Newcastle lifted the Inter-Cities Fairs Cup in 1969. He scored some spectacular goals during United's early years of European competition. Although not the tallest of players, he was still a dangerous attacker in the air.

weren't in the competition just to make up numbers.

A crowd of more than 46,000 saw the big names of Dutch football fall completely flat as United raced to a 4–0 first-leg advantage. Feyenoord were simply hammered out of sight and the result could easily have been 8–0, the woodwork saving the visitors on three occasions! It was a great team performance by the Magpies against a side that was on its way to winning the league championship in Holland that season and to claim the European Champions' Cup 12 months' later.

Young Geoff Allen, playing on the wing, was the tormentor-in-chief in that historic first encounter. He had a field day, while Jim Scott opened Newcastle's Euro account after big Wyn Davies – the key figure in United's side – started a move which saw Allen fire in a ball across the face of goal for Scott to side-foot home. Bryan Robson, Tommy Gibb and Welsh international Davies completed the scoring and the Magpies marched off in triumph to a standing ovation. The Tyneside crowd had received their first taste of European football – and loved it.

Next in line were two more seasoned foreign clubs – Sporting Lisbon and Real Zaragoza – and both felt the force of Newcastle's danger-men up front, Wyn

Davies and Bryan Robson, a little-and-large duo who had a great understanding. Portuguese outfit Vitoria Setubal went the same way, beaten 6–4 on aggregate in the quarter-final. That success took United to an epic clash with Glasgow Rangers, a two-legged semi-final which had just about everything.

A crowd of more than 75,000 – the biggest ever to watch United, apart from cup finals – congregated at Ibrox Park for the first contest, and United gave them something to remember, displaying character and determination typical of their spirited line-up. In a rearguard action they came back to Tyneside with a 0–0 draw. Goalkeeper Willie McFaul was everyone's hero after the Northern Ireland international made headlines with a stunning penalty save in the first half.

A sell-out 60,000 attendance witnessed the return fixture and the events of that game were certainly worth waiting for, although probably not for the football! The drama, tension and incident which took place with the players off the field completely overshadowed United's fine 2–0 victory in a very tough and physical game which was more like the Battle of Bannockburn than a European semi-final.

The spark that lit the fuse for these incidents was the tremendous 77th-minute volleyed goal scored by

Jackie Sinclair which secured the game for United. The goal cased unfortunate fan reaction and led to the players leaving the pitch for 17 minutes. When play finally restarted the atmosphere was very hostile but the Magpies kept their nerve to win the tie, 2–0 on aggregate. In the club's first season in European competition, Newcastle were through to the Final.

United's dogged side, criticized in some quarters for lack of finesse, had made it. But their eleven, led by Scottish international Bobby Moncur, possessed tremendous character and spirit. During May and June of 1969 they met Hungarians Ujpest Dosza, a team several judges rated as one of the best club sides on the Continent.

After a terrific 3–0 victory on Tyneside in front of another capacity crowd, the Black-and-Whites were favourites to lift the trophy. Skipper Moncur led from the front in a brilliant performance. The central defender netted twice on the day, his first senior goals in almost 10 years as a pro at St James' Park! And he wasn't finished, either, as the Hungarians felt the Moncur boot again just when United needed a goal in an amazing second leg.

In the Hungarian capital of Budapest, Newcastle took a hammering from the Magyars during the opening 45 minutes. Ujpest tore into United and clawed two goals of the 3–0 deficit back by the interval. Bene and Gorocs had Newcastle in all sorts of trouble, and things looked bleak for the Magpies as they went into the dressing-room at half-time.

It needed an inspirational team talk from boss Joe Harvey to spark a United fightback in the second half. Once again it was centre-half Moncur – having got the taste for scoring – who lashed in the all-important goal which caused Hungarian heads to drop. In a brilliant second-half display, United went on to score twice more, eventually winning 6–2 on aggregate. The Inter-Cities Fairs Cup was on its way to Tyneside.

Scoring hero Bobby Moncur has a free header in the first leg of the Fairs Cup Final against Ujpest Dosza.

Trophy Defence

Newcastle fans just could not wait for the next instalment of the club's European adventures. The following season, 1969–70, they did well again, reaching the quarter-final after toppling Dundee United, FC Porto and Southampton. In the last eight they faced another of Europe's aristocrats, RSC Anderlecht from Belgium. Again Newcastle looked as though they were going to reach the semi-final, but leading on aggregate and with only a few minutes remaining on the clock in the decisive leg at St James' Park, a defensive slip allowed the Belgians to fire a shot past McFaul. The crowd of 59,000 was stunned into silence. United were out on the away goals rule.

United took time to recover from that bitter defeat, but it was soon a memory when Newcastle were drawn against the might of Internationale from Milan in the first round of the 1970–71 competition. And just as a bonus, several of the Italian stars had played in the recently completed World Cup in Mexico: names such as Facchetti, Burgnich, Mazzola and Boninsegna.

After a creditable 1–1 draw in the San Siro, Newcastle won a thrilling encounter 2–0 on home turf. United played the Italians off the park that evening, and, for their sins, the Latins almost tore United limb from limb. Even referee Minnoy was given the treatment: Inter's goalkeeper Vieri floored him with a right hook and was sent off for his trouble!

That sparkling performance was all for nothing, however, as United went out in the next round to unknown Hungarians Pesci Dosza on penalties. It turned out to be a long wait for the next European tie: not until the 1977–78 season did the Magpies qualify for European action again. Newcastle were then a side struggling in the old Division One and, having taken care of Dublin's Bohemians, were matched with French club Bastia.

Little was expected of the relegation-bound Magpies and that's how it turned out over the tie. Bastia boasted Dutch World Cup ace Johnny Rep, a striker of the highest quality, and he tormented Newcastle as the Magpies fell 3–1 at St James' Park – the club's first defeat on home soil.

John Beresford scores his and United's second goal in their Champions' League debut against Croatia Zagreb at St James' Park in August 1997.

Out of the Wilderness

That exit saw United in the wilderness for over a decade. Not until Kevin Keegan led United into third place in the Premiership in 1993–94 did the Magpies get a sniff of European football again. Newcastle's new Continental exploits began in Belgium against Royal Antwerp, and they certainly created an impression. Keegan's entertaining and attacking policy was perfectly displayed as the Magpies destroyed the Belgians 5–0 on the night and 10–2 on aggregate! But against a much stronger Athletic Bilbao line-up in the next round, United paid the penalty for being naïve. Leading 3–0 in the first meeting at St James' Park, the Magpies should have had the tie wrapped up, but they relaxed their grip on the match and allowed the Spanish club to score two late, crucial, away goals. It spelt disaster and elimination from the UEFA Cup.

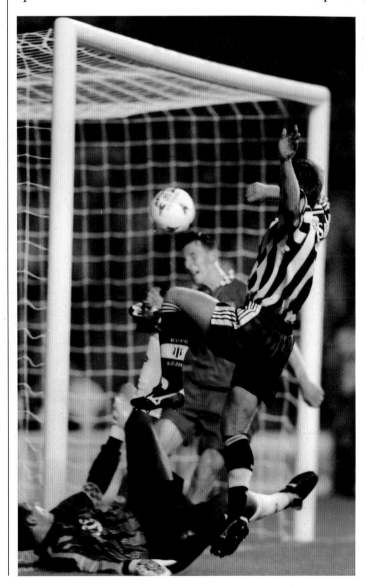

In 1996–97 Newcastle were one of the favourites to reach the final of the same competition. They took care of Swedish outfit Halmstads comfortably, then faced Ferencvaros, one of Europe's experienced big names. A return to Budapest saw United snatch two vital away goals, while a five-star performance back on Tyneside – especially from Tino Asprilla and David Ginola – secured them a place in the next round. Newcastle reached the quarter-final by taking care of French outfit Metz, but they faced another club much fancied for the trophy, Monaco. United were struck by an injury jinx to key strikers Alan Shearer and Les Ferdinand for both matches, and also had to cope without their top European scorer, Asprilla, because of suspension. It was a handicap too great to overcome, the silky Mediterranean club winning 1–0 at St James' Park and 4–0 on aggregate.

And so to United's debut in the European Champions' League. Newcastle are fast becoming one of the Continent's top clubs and are hot on the trail of a second European trophy.

Qualifying Seasons

Qualifying Seasons

Inter-Cities Fairs Cup:	1968–69, 1969–70, 1970–71
UEFA Cup;	1977–78, 1994–95, 1996–97
European Champions' League:	1997–98

Biggest Victory
5–0, vs. Royal Antwerp (a) 1994–95

Heaviest Defeat
0–3, vs. Monaco (a) 1996–97

Top Home Crowds
59,309, vs. Anderlecht 1969–70
59,303, vs. Glasgow Rangers 1968–69
59,234, vs. Ujpest Dosza 1968–69

Top Gate
75,580, vs. Glasgow Rangers (a) 1968–69

Most Appearances
24 games, by W McFaul, B Robson, T Gibb & W Davies

Most Goals
10, by W Davies

Peter Beardsley in full flight against Athletic Bilbao during the 1994 UEFA Cup tie.

United have the Rangers defence at full stretch in the second leg of the Inter-Cities Fairs Cup semi-final. The all-British semi-final proved to be a remarkable and passion-filled meeting. Newcastle reached the Final by winning the second leg at St James' Park 2–0, after a goalless draw at Ibrox Park.

Newcastle United 2 (0)
Rangers 0 (0)

Inter-Cities Fairs Cup Semi-Final
21 May 1969, at St James' Park

The first leg of this all-British European contest, played in front of 75,580 fans at Ibrox Park in Glasgow, ended level at 0–0, so there was everything to play for in the decisive match on Tyneside. And it was an England–Scotland clash that made headlines throughout Europe. The tension surrounding the game meant that neither side played to form and there were too many fouls and petty stoppages. It was a dour struggle and a long way from being a classic. But, for the capacity all-ticket crowd, it was a fixture that would never be forgotten.

Tackles were rough and fierce, and it took courage to hold on to the ball for any length of time. The first half ended in stalemate with few clear-cut chances in either goalmouth. However, in the second period events changed rapidly. Wyn Davies and Jackie Sinclair were proving difficult to handle and the Magpies came into the game strongly.

In the 52nd minute Jim Scott received a defence-splitting pass from Tommy Gibb. He left Rangers defender Mathieson wallowing in his slipstream and hit a fierce shot across German goalkeeper Neef high into the net.

The deadlock had been broken and United put the pressure on the Scottish rearguard. Only 13 minutes from time, the Magpies clinched a place in the Fairs Cup final when Ollie Burton flighted a long free kick into the Rangers box. Welshman Wyn Davies jumped for it, got a knock down and Jackie Sinclair caught the ball on the volley to bulge the net.

The goal certainly decided the tie and hordes of visiting fans vented their frustration by invading the pitch. There had been a couple of brief disruptions earlier in the evening, but this time the match was held up for 17 minutes. When play restarted, Newcastle had to be careful that the passion off the field did not deflect them from the task in hand, that of reaching the Final.

As it was, the match died as a contest after the long stoppage. The Rangers players were clearly stunned by the incident and had little heart for a fightback. United went through to their first European final.

Inter-Cities Fairs Cup Semi-final, 21 May 1969

United: McFaul, Craig, Clark, Gibb, Burton, Moncur, Scott, Robson, Davies, Arentoft, Sinclair.	Rangers: Neef, Johansen, Mathieson, Greig, McKinnon (Provan), Smith, Henderson, Penman, Stein, Johnston, Persson.
Subs not used: Hope, Foggon, Craggs.	
Goals: Scott (52), Sinclair (77).	**Att:** 59,303

Newcastle United 2 (1)
Internazionale Milan 0 (0)
European Fairs Cup Round 1
30 September 1970, at St James' Park

Newcastle United were given little chance in the 1970–71 tournament when they were drawn with European giants Inter Milan in the first stage of the competition. The Magpies, however, outshone their more illustrious opponents in both legs of this classic.

United almost snatched a well-earned victory at the San Siro stadium before a late equalizer rescued Inter from a single-goal defeat. In front of a near-capacity crowd at St James' Park, the Magpies went for the Italians from the kick-off. They attacked constantly and could have been ahead in the opening 15 minutes. Playing in an unfamiliar all-red strip, Newcastle had their Italian visitors panicking and, after 29 minutes, deservedly, went in front. A Bryan Robson corner was met perfectly by skipper Bobby Moncur and the ball hurtled into the net from a glorious header.

A minute later it was nearly 2–0, but Inter's goal-keeper Vieri collected the ball just as Wyn Davies was about to pounce. United's Number Nine challenged Vieri, and a fracas followed, after which a free kick was awarded to Newcastle in the Inter box. In the ensuing argument, referee Minnoy was first pushed and then punched to the ground by the irate Italian keeper. He recovered after aid from the United trainer, while three policemen controlled the angry visitors. Vieri was sent off and the game was then held up for another four minutes as arguments restarted.

From that controversial moment, Inter resorted to almost any foul tactic to stop United, and big Wyn Davies – whose robust style was impossible for the Italians to handle – was given some horrendous treatment in a most unsavoury way. At one stage the police were again obliged to come on to the pitch to restrain some of Inter players who had gone too far.

To their credit, Newcastle kept cool and rarely retaliated, preferring to keep up their incessant attack. They rattled the bar twice, the second time in the 70th minute after Keith Dyson had headed on to the wood-work: this time Davies followed up and netted with a brave diving header. For his trouble, he was then kicked and struck in the face by Inter defenders.

United were a perfect advertisement for English football. In spite of everything Newcastle had played brilliantly against some of the world's finest.

European Fairs Cup Round 1, 30 September 1970

United: McFaul, Craig, Clark, Gibb, Burton, Moncur, Robson, Dyson, Davies, Arentoft, Young.
Subs not used: Hope, Guthrie, Elliott.

Inter Milan: Vieri, Righetti, Facchetti, Bellugi, Giubertoni, Cella, Jair, Fabbian, Boninsegna, Archilli (Bordon), Corso.

Goals: Moncur (29), Davies (70).　**Att:** 56,495

Royal Antwerp 0 (0)
Newcastle United 5 (3)
UEFA Cup Round 1
13 September 1994, at Bosuil Stadium

Royal Antwerp were not among the big boys of European soccer, but they were still a respected and experienced side from Belgium. Newcastle not only defeated them with ease, but at times toyed with their opponents in a display which ranks as one of the Magpies' best modern performances.

United got off to a marvellous start when Robert Lee ghosted into the penalty area and headed in a John Beresford cross immediately from the kick-off.

Antwerp were stunned and didn't recover. They went 2–0 down after only nine minutes, when that man Lee again stole into the box and converted another cross with a leap – this time beating his own man, Andy Cole, to the ball!

Newcastle's passing game was on song. Their interchanges were delightful and Scott Sellars finished off a brilliant move from an Andy Cole pass. The Belgians did go close after the interval but Pavel Srnicek played a part with good saves. Then Robert Lee grabbed his hat-trick with his third header of the evening. A passing movement found Marc Hottiger and his good cross was met by United's midfielder.

United now started to mesmerize their opponents, and Steve Watson – on as substitute for Peter Beardsley, who had just returned from injury – scored the goal of the night. Newcastle's young utility player started on a run that saw him go round three defenders and then goalkeeper Svilar before slipping the ball into the net to make it 5–0.

It had been a fantastic night in their first European fixture for almost 20 years. The Magpies had answered those critics who had suggested that Newcastle could not play their famously entertaining brand football in this competition. The resounding answer was: Oh, yes, they could!

UEFA Cup Round 1, 13 September 1994

Royal Antwerp: Svilar, Vangompel, Smidts, Emmerechts, Broeckaert, Kulcsar, Porte, Kiekens, Zohar (Monteiro), Severeyns, Godfraid.
Subs not used: Van der Straeten, Van Rethy, Moukrim, Aloisi.

Att: 19,700

United: Srnicek, Hottiger, Beresford, Venison, Peacock, Albert, Fox, Lee, Cole (Jeffrey), Beardsley (Watson), Sellars.
Subs not used: Hooper, Howey, Elliott.

Goals: Lee (1, 9, 50), Sellars (39), Watson (78).

Right: Andy Cole is airborne against Antwerp. Below: Rob Lee lashes his second goal in Antwerp after just 9 minutes.

Newcastle United 4 (1)
Ferencvaros 0 (0)

UEFA Cup Round Two 29 October 1996, St James' Park

The champions of Hungary were 3–2 up after the first leg of this entertaining tie, but when they landed at St James' Park, Ferencvaros felt the overwhelming might of United's attack. Manager Kevin Keegan fielded an adventurous line-up, with only three defenders on the

pitch at the start, and the tactics worked like a dream.

The first half was 45 minutes of one-way traffic on the Hungarians' goal, and only some desperate defending stopped David Ginola, Tino Asprilla and Les Ferdinand getting United on level terms. They even survived a 22nd-minute penalty when Tino turned quickly in the box, only to be felled. But Peter Beardsley struck the post, and many thought it was going to be one of those frustrating evenings!

But destiny was about to take a hand, as 19 minutes later Philippe Albert headed down a Keith Gillespie corner and opportunist Asprilla was on the mark to sweep the ball home. The Colombian was again in the right place in the second half, collecting a Darren Peacock knock-down and guiding a shot beyond the advancing keeper, Szeiler, to put Newcastle 2–0 up on the night, and 4–3 ahead on aggregate.

A third goal was needed to secure the tie, and it came out of the top drawer. Gillespie fired in a corner which was cleared to the edge of the box. David Ginola, who had sparkled all evening, controlled the ball on his chest, lifted it over a challenge and then struck a looping volley into the top right-hand corner of the Hungarians' net. In terms of individual skill, it was one of the best goals ever seen at Gallowgate.

Beardsley, Asprilla and Lee could have found the net too, all three players coming agonizingly close. Then, on time, Warren Barton hit a low cross and Les Ferdinand slid the ball into the net to make the score 4–0, and 6–3 on aggregate. It had been as good a show as anyone could have wished to see.

Left: The Ferencvaros defence is left helpless by Faustino Asprilla in Newcastle's 4–0 second-leg demolition of the Hungarians at St James' Park. Below: With defence flat-footed, Les Ferdinand sends Ferencvaros goalkeeper Szeiler the wrong way as he shoots for goal.

UEFA Cup Round 2, 29 October 1996

United: Srnicek, Peacock, Albert, Elliott, Batty, Gillespie (Barton), Ginola, Lee, Beardsley, Asprilla, Ferdinand.
Subs not used: Watson, Kitson, Clark, Hislop.

Goals: Asprilla (41, 58), Ginola (64), Ferdinand (90).

Ferencvaros: Szeiler, Telek, Kuznyecov (Arany), Hrutka, Nyilas, Szucs, Miriuta (Zavadszky), Jagodics, Nagy N, Horvath (Hollo), Nicsenko.
Subs not used: Nagy T, Simon.

Att: 35,740

Up for the Cup

To many supporters the tension and elation that can be generated from cup ties is what football is all about. The do-or-die knock-out has an enchantment fans love.

In modern times, Newcastle United have not enjoyed much success in either the FA Cup or Football League Cup. Yet the Magpies have a proud tradition as one of the big names of cup football, especially in that magical competition, the FA Cup. Only Manchester United, Tottenham and Aston Villa can better United's six victories, and only Arsenal, Everton and the Reds from Old Trafford have been to more finals. And alongside much FA Cup glory, Newcastle have created plenty of controversial news too, be it a giant-killing shock or a talking-point victory against clubs of equal status.

Crystal Palace sorcery

The Magpies' first taste of success in the FA Cup nearly ended almost as soon as it began. In the 1904–05 season Plymouth Argyle – then a Southern League club – took the Tynesiders to three hard-fought games before a couple of goals at a neutral Woolwich Arsenal stadium sent United on their way to the Final.

Newcastle's appearance in that season's final at the old Crystal Palace enclosure at Sydenham saw the Magpies face Aston Villa in what was the Midlands club's fifth final. Newcastle were League Champions-elect, but their visits to London in those pre-Wembley days were to be plagued by poor performances and bad luck. Villa cruised to a 2–0 victory through goals from their ace forward, Harry Hampton.

United were the dominant force in the country during this era, and in 1906 they reached the Final for the second year running. However, once more they were unable to display their obvious talent in the final and lost again. What should have been a showpiece of the season turned out to be a non-event. Everton, the Magpies' great rivals in these years, won the contest with what was described as the only worthwhile moment of the match – a 75th-minute goal from Sandy Young.

Two years later, Newcastle fell again at the Crystal Palace. They even faced Division Two opposition this time, in the shape of Wolverhampton Wanderers, but couldn't find their form. However, Newcastle did play more convincingly than on their previous two visits to the final, and had England winger Jackie Rutherford not missed two early chances the FA Cup might have ended up on Tyneside rather than in the Midlands.

Newcastle's possession-based, carpet-style football was swamped by the physical approach of Wolves; and despite United's bright opening, they netted twice by half-time. Jimmy Howie pulled a goal back for the Magpies, but then a hesitation by Jimmy Lawrence allowed Harrison in to wrap the game up for Wolves.

Ignoring this set-back, Newcastle kept going in their bid to land the FA Cup. The famous trophy did finally come to Tyneside in 1910, although United had first to get away from the hypnotic trance of the Crystal Palace. Against a rugged Barnsley outfit, a Rutherford equalizer in the 83rd minute earned Newcastle a replay. It was a controversial goal, with the Tykes claiming that Rutherford was offside when he headed home a Higgins free kick.

In the replay, United now played at Goodison Park, home of Everton. The surroundings suited the Magpies far better and their performance was much more polished. Mixing tough football with their celebrated brand of classical soccer, they came out 2–0 winners and took

Newcastle first won the FA Cup in 1910. Note the club mascot, Rex, a black and white Great Dane dog.

the Cup back to Newcastle for the first time.

Barnsley's goal had some miraculous escapes in the first half and it took United some time to break the deadlock. But star centre-forward Albert Shepherd showed his England form when he powered his way through to score with a fast, low shot. Newcastle's second, killer goal came from the penalty spot – the first penalty ever awarded in an FA Cup final. Skipper Colin Veitch handed the ball to Shepherd who blasted the ball home to cheers from delighted Geordies.

The Edwardian years were great times for Newcastle United, and in 1911 they were back for their fifth Cup final in only seven attempts. But Albert Shepherd, such an important figure in the club's plans, was injured just before the Final and was to be sidelined for several months. He was irreplaceable. And more bad news followed when another key player, Scottish international playmaker Peter McWilliam, was also put out of the final by another injury. The Crystal Palace bogey had struck before Newcastle had even entered the arena.

The Tynesiders' opponents were Bradford City, placed above United in the Division One table, and a dull, lifeless final resulted in a dull, lifeless 0–0 scoreline. At Old Trafford in the replay United's goalkeeper Jimmy Lawrence – who holds the club record for the most appearances – misjudged a ball and allowed Jimmy Speirs to net with one of the softest Cup Final goals ever. It was enough to send the trophy to Bradford rather than to Newcastle.

Although United were regular visitors to the final in the years leading up to the First World War, they were also the victims of a spot of FA Cup giant-killing. In 1907 they fell at the first hurdle to a non-League club. And guess who they were? Crystal Palace! The hoodoo was really cemented when the Londoners – including a line-up of several players from the North-East and ex-Newcastle men – toppled United at St James' Park through a single goal. It was one of the greatest feats in the history of the FA Cup, for United were crowned Football League Champions at the end of the season!

That Wembley Feeling

The inter-war years proved happier times for Newcastle in FA Cup finals. In 1924 the Magpies reached the Final again, but this time United didn't have to face another 90 minutes at Sydenham in South London. English football had a new national stadium, at Wembley, on the other side of the capital. And Newcastle's showmen took immediately to the vast new arena.

In only the second final to be played at the celebrated stadium, United met Aston Villa once more. It was a match that lived in the memory for years. Goalkeeper Bill Bradley was a late replacement for regular Sandy Mutch, and the stand-in played his heart out as Newcastle won 2–0. On the soft, greasy

pitch, an entertaining and evenly-balanced match developed. Chances went past the post or were well-saved at both ends, and just when everyone was predicting extra-time, Newcastle hit Villa not once, but twice, netting two quick strikes in the last seven minutes through Neil Harris and Stan Seymour.

When Newcastle embarked on the FA Cup trail in 1932 they could not possibly have imagined the storm which would surround their eventual success. Along with England's 1966 World Cup Final goal which bounced in off the crossbar, Jack Allen's effort against Arsenal is rated as the most controversial goal in the history of Wembley Stadium.

Arsenal were the great team of the Thirties. On paper, they had enough stars to swamp Newcastle's solid, above-average line-up. A classic final resulted, with the Magpies matching their more illustrious counterparts man for man. Fast, flowing football and narrow escapes were witnessed before Gunners winger Bob John put Arsenal ahead.

Then came a 38th-minute Newcastle equalizer that had the nation talking for weeks. United's centre-half Dave Davidson intercepted a Hapgood interchange and sent Jimmy Richardson flying down the wing in pursuit of a long, raking pass. Richardson stretched for it and whipped the ball from the bye-line into the penalty area for Jack Allen to crash the ball into the Londoners' net. From that moment United were the better side, and it was no injustice when Allen scored the winner after beating two defenders. Before the end Richardson had another good chance, but hit the Gunners' post.

It was not until after the game that a huge rumpus started, when newspaper photographs seemed to show that the ball had crossed the line before Richardson centred it for United's equalizer. Some of the pictures were from deceiving angles, but the Movietone newsreel also appeared to indicate that the ball had gone out of play. Yet the referee, Percy Harper, was adamant that the goal was a fair one. Newcastle were worthy winners of what has been known ever since as the "Over The Line Final".

Newcastle skipper Frank Hudspeth walks off the Wembley turf in friendly conversation with a policeman. United beat Aston Villa 2–0 in the 1924 FA Cup Final, the second year the Stadium hosted the match. Hudspeth appeared in 472 games for the Magpies, the most by an outfield player.

Newcastle's FA Cup Final team is presented to H.M. King George V on the Wembley pitch before the 1932 match against Arsenal. The Magpies lifted the Cup for a third time after a controversial 2–1 win.

Fifties Treble

Newcastle's side of the 1950s goes down in history as one of the finest of all FA Cup sides. In 1951 they recorded the first of three fabulous Wembley victories in a five-year period. They felled Blackpool in that year, a side crammed with top players including the legendary Stanley Matthews. The nation wanted a Blackpool victory for Matthews' sake, but instead saw a United success and Jackie Milburn grabbing all the headlines. It was "Wor Jackie" who wrote his name on that final with two superlative goals, the first a breakaway effort and the second a humdinger of a shot from 30 yards.

Arsenal renewed their rivalry with the Magpies a year later in 1952. United's path to Wembley had been a very difficult one, with games against four clubs from the top six in the first division and only one home tie. But the club's fantastic spirit at the time delivered another final appearance in style.

The Gunners were going for the double that season but United's Chilean international, George Robledo, dashed Arsenal's hopes with a single winning goal in

"Bobby Dazzler" Mitchell shoots inside Bert Trautmann's near post in the 1955 FA Cup Final.

the 84th minute. Bobby Mitchell, a wizard on United's left wing, dribbled up the bye-line and sent over a looping cross which was met by the powerful Robledo, who headed home off the post. Newcastle lifted the trophy and equalled Blackburn Rovers' 60-year-old record of winning the FA Cup in successive seasons.

In 1955 Newcastle made what was then a record 10th appearance in the Final. Their opponents were Manchester City, who were marshalled by the deep-lying centre-forward Don Revie and his famous "Revie Plan". Once more Jackie Milburn was the man of the moment, and in double-quick time – this after not being selected to play by manager Doug Livingstone, but then reinstated by director Stan Seymour!

The game began sensationally, Milburn putting Newcastle in front after only 45 seconds with a flying header from a corner. It was the quickest FA Cup Final goal at Wembley until 1997, when Roberto Di Matteo netted for Chelsea against Middlesbrough. In a fine match, Manchester City came back and Bobby Johnstone equalized. But then Newcastle stepped up a gear and Mitchell and George Hannah made sure captain Jimmy Scoular would be climbing the Wembley steps to receive some silverware once again.

Keegan's Double

Since those heady days of the Fifties, United have failed to bring the FA Cup trophy back to Tyneside. For almost 20 years Newcastle rarely threatened to have a decent run in the famous competition, and more often than not Magpie fans were pulling their hair out at below-par performances against lesser opposition. As a Division Two club they lost to non-League Bedford Town in 1964, and worse followed in 1972. Newcastle were by then one of the top division's best sides, with Malcolm Macdonald in attack and Bobby Moncur in defence. But they were the victim of another giant-killer, in a tie that rivals Crystal Palace's success back in 1907. Hereford United, who were then a non-League club too, took care of the Magpies after a replay – and it was shown to millions watching on television into the bargain!

Two years later Newcastle did repay their fans for that embarrasment by going all the way to Wembley for what turned out to be their last FA Cup Final appearance to date. It was then a record 11th final for United, who faced the might of a formidable

Newcastle's most recent FA Cup Final appearance came back in 1974 when Liverpool triumphed 3–0. Their two-goal hero that day was a man who became a legend on Tyneside, Kevin Keegan.

Liverpool side which included Kevin Keegan. And it was he, the future Newcastle hero, who destroyed the Black-and-Whites with two goals to power the Reds to a comfortable 3–0 victory. Newcastle never got into the game and were both overawed and outplayed.

Nearly 25 years on from that day in 1974, the Magpies are still striving to add their name to the FA Cup again. Since they gained the status of a Premier League superclub, there has been much speculation that United would be soon at Wembley again. They are among the favourites to succeed each year and reached the sixth round in 1995. A slice of FA Cup fortune is all the Magpies need.

Wembley bound in 1976 (from left): Craig, Nattrass, Kennedy and Barrowclough celebrate.

League Cup bogey

The early days of the Football League Cup were clouded with apathy from a number of the top clubs; some, in fact, didn't even bother to compete during the early years of the Sixties. Newcastle United didn't really take the competition seriously for several years, and not surprisingly their performances did not set their fans alight. And when the Magpies did start to look at the League Cup as a trophy worth winning, they found it increasingly difficult to get past the early rounds.

In fact, lower-division opposition loved to draw Newcastle as they knew they always had a chance of winning. The competition hung over the Magpies like a shroud. Colchester United, Leyton Orient, Bournemouth and Peterborough United all inflicted painful defeats on the Tynesiders. Division Four Lincoln City added further insult by winning in 1967 and Bristol Rovers did likewise three years later.

Even with a Wembley final and a European place on offer, results kept going the wrong way for Newcastle: that is, until the 1974–75 season, when at last the League Cup bogey was thrown off for a brief period. They defeated Nottingham Forest after a replay, then won convincingly at Queens Park Rangers, 4–0, thanks to a stunning Macdonald hat-trick. Fulham went down 3–0 yet, with a Wembley appointment just around the corner, lowly Chester arrived on the scene to dump Newcastle out of the Cup. Another disaster: but at least the Magpies had progressed to the latter stages of the competition for the first time, and the following year they went all the way, just narrowly failing to lift the trophy.

In 1975–76, Newcastle started a Wembley run with a convincing 6–0 win over Southport and then success

against Bristol Rovers. QPR were again beaten in an exciting game at St James' Park, and Notts County were taken care of through a freak own goal by their 'keeper! An epic semi-final with Tottenham followed, with the club going through to Wembley in front of a crowd of nearly 50,000.

Newcastle met Manchester City in the Final, and despite the effects of a 'flu bug on United, the Magpies battled hard to uphold their honour in an exciting end-to-end contest. Although Alan Gowling equalized City's opener, a spectacular overhead kick from Newcastle-born Dennis Tueart in the second half sent the cup to Maine Road.

Newcastle Cup RECORD

Record FA Cup Victory
9–0 vs. Southport (a) February 1932

Record Football League Cup Victory
6–0 vs. Southport (h) September 1975
7–1 vs. Notts County (a) October 1993

Heaviest FA Cup Defeat
1–7 vs. Aston Villa (a) February 1895

Heaviest Football League Cup Defeat
2–7 vs. Manchester United (a) October 1976

Biggest FA Cup Attendance at St James' Park
67,596 vs. Bolton Wanderers 1950–51

Biggest Football League Cup Attendance at St James' Park
49,902 vs. Tottenham Hotspur 1975–76

Most Goals in FA Cup Football
23 goals by Jackie Milburn

Most Goals in Football League Cup
12 goals by Malcolm Macdonald

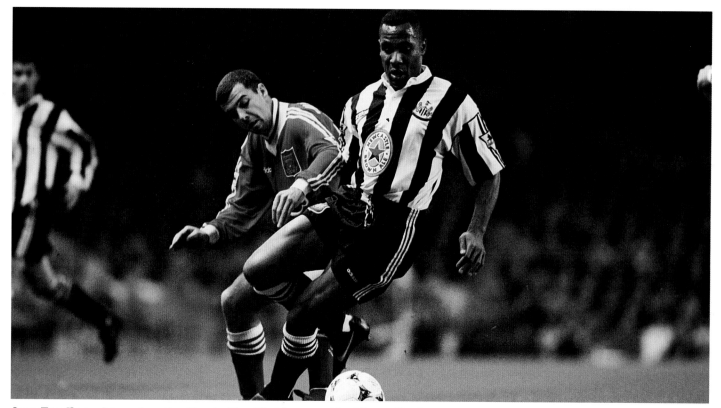

Les Ferdinand tussles for the ball with Liverpool's Steve Harkness during Newcastle's 1–0 victory at Anfield in the 4th round of the 1995–96 Coca-Cola Cup. United lost to Arsenal in the quarter-final.

Since then, the League Cup bogey has returned to haunt United. Bury, Oxford United, Bradford City and Watford have all claimed a Newcastle scalp. So, once again, has Peterborough. Recently, the Magpies have put together some impressive results, no longer easy meat for the lower-division clubs. They hit Notts County for 11 goals over two legs, and crushed Bristol City 5–0 and Stoke City 4–0, both away from St James' Park. And, when they took care of Liverpool 1–0 at Anfield in the 1995–96 season – thanks to a brilliant Steve Watson effort – the Toon Army reckoned the bogey had well and truly been dumped. But Arsenal made sure it hadn't, and Newcastle were no closer to getting to Wembley and securing a League Cup trophy.

Newcastle United 6 (2)
Fulham 0 (0)

FA Cup semi-final
28 March 1908, at Anfield

FA Cup semi-finals are usually tense, close and dramatic affairs. Not so United's 1908 clash with Londoners Fulham. In this clash of the mighty versus the minnow Newcastle, the reigning Football League Champions, steamrollered League new-boys Fulham aside with consummate ease. The Magpies were on brilliant form and cruised into the final, setting a record for a FA Cup semi-final scoreline in the process.

The Craven Cottage club had achieved something of a sensation back in 1908 when they reached the semi-final by knocking out both Manchester teams, but when matched against United's international-packed team Fulham were totally outclassed. Even without elegant Scottish midfielder Peter McWilliam, ruled out with an ankle injury, the Tynesiders were still in command from start to finish.

The Anfield pitch was drying out after an overnight downpour and, from the start, United went at their London opponents. Fulham's goal had a number of close shaves before Bill Appleyard opened the scoring, heading into the net following a free-kick awarded after Alec Gardner had been fouled on a solo run. Then England winger Jackie Rutherford went clear on the flank, crossed, and a dummy by Appleyard let in Jimmy Howie. The schemer's shot sped past 'keeper Leslie Skene and United were 2–0 ahead at half-time.

After the interval Fulham disintegrated. Gardner scored a soft goal after a mistake by full-back Ross; Rutherford came back, tricking two defenders before scoring with a great shot to give United a 4–0 lead.

Bill Appleyard (centre) powers the ball over the line to open the scoring in the 1908 semi-final.

Then big Bill Appleyard collided with Skene who – in the days when referees did not protect goalkeepers from charging forwards– was bundled over heavily and left a passenger.

With their 'keeper hobbling around, Fulham had little hope. A cross-shot from Howie gave Newcastle their fifth goal and then star man Rutherford, who had enjoyed a field-day all afternoon, galloped away, slipped past two challenges and drove home another goal to make the score 6–0. After that Newcastle sat back, played exhibition football – and looked forward to the FA Cup Final.

FA Cup Semi-Final, 28 March 1908

United: Lawrence, McCracken, Pudan, Gardner, Veitch, Willis, Rutherford, Howie, Appleyard, Speedie, Wilson.

Fulham: Skene, Ross, Lindsay, Collins, Morrison, Goldie, Hogan, Dalrymple, Harrison, Millington, Moucher.

United's goalscorers:
Appleyard (32), Howie (40, 74), Gardner (58), Rutherford (71, 89).   **Att:** 45,571

Newcastle United 5 (3)
Derby County 3 (2)
FA Cup Round Two, Third Replay
13 February 1924, at St James' Park

Newcastle United's meeting with Derby County in the 1923–24 FA Cup is one of the longest on record in the competition. It took the Magpies four games and 420 minutes of football to dispose of the Rams and progress en route to lifting the trophy that year. Almost every one of those minutes was action-packed, and the deciding match at St James' Park – after United had won the choice of venue by the toss of a coin – was to prove quite sensational.

County, third in Division Two and the Football League's leading goalgetters, held Division One United with three 2–2 draws, at the Baseball Ground, St James' Park and neutral Burnden Park. And United were only saved by a Stan Seymour's equalizer in the last minute of extra-time at Bolton.

In the fourth meeting Derby were handicapped by the loss of their potent winger, George Thornewell, but it appeared to matter little as the Rams took command in the opening exchanges. United were rocked as Derby stormed into a 1–0 lead through centre-forward Randolph Galloway. St James' Park was silenced. Newcastle needed something special and in true FA Cup tradition Neil Harris – who was later to lead Scotland's forward line – came to the Black-and-Whites' rescue.

Newcastle rolled up their sleeves and turned the 1–0 deficit into a 2–1 advantage, only for Galloway to equalize. But Harris chose that afternoon to net a magnificent 24-minute hat-trick that stunned the Rams and had Newcastle's fans going wild with delight. By half-time United were back ahead by the odd goal in five.

Neil Harris, Newcastle's Scottish international centre-forward, netted a spectacular hat-trick in the 5–3 defeat of Derby County at St James' Park in 1924.

FA Cup Round 2, 13 February 1924

United: Mutch, Hampson, Hudspeth, Mooney, Spencer, Gibson, Low, Cowan, Harris, McDonald, Seymour.

Derby County: Olney, Chandler, Crilly, McIntyre, Thoms, Plackett, Keetley, Whitehouse, Galloway, Storer, Murphy.

United's goalscorers: Harris (20, 32, 44), Seymour (53), Cowan (66).

County's goalscorers: Galloway (15, 40), Storer (60),

Att: 32,496

Newcastle went further in front after half-time, when Stan Seymour netted within eight minutes of the restart. But Derby were not finished; and, as they had proved in earlier games, were going to fight to the very last minute. On the hour Harry Storer pulled a goal back, and with County piling on the pressure for the equalizer there were visions of extra time again, and even a fifth meeting. This time, though, United held out and broke away to claim another goal through Willie Cowan.

Len White scored twice in the epic FA Cup tie with Manchester City at Maine Road in 1957.

Manchester City 4 (3)
Newcastle United 5 (0)
FA Cup Round 3 Replay
9 January 1957, at Maine Road

United's victory at Maine Road ranks as one of the club's finest-ever cup wins. Manchester City were FA Cup-holders, while the Magpies had recently completed a treble of Wembley appearances, including a victory over City two years earlier. The pairing of United and City was the pick of the third-round draw, and the tie lived up to its billing.

After a 1–1 draw at St James' Park in which City had the better of the game, Newcastle went into the replay without the considerable talents of Jackie Milburn. In stepped youngster Alex Tait, a part-timer who was training to become a schoolteacher. And the stand-in centre-forward proved to be United's saviour at a crucial period in a terrific contest.

On a muddy pitch City went at the Geordies from the kick-off and United found themselves 3–0 down within a short period. Bob Stokoe netted an own-goal trying to clear the ball over his own bar, then Bobby Johnstone scored with a fine header from a free kick. A minute later Fagan latched on to a glorious, defence-splitting pass from McAdams, and City were three goals in front and seemingly destined to win the tie.

United's cause looked hopeless. However, the FA Cup is such a special competition that players try much harder at times like this and the Magpies' fighting spirit, so evident in this era, was soon to put Newcastle back in the game.

United clawed a goal back through a Tommy Casey penalty kick when Bill Curry was sent tumbling. That fired up the Magpies, and it was now City's turn to feel the strain. With 16 minutes remaining Alex Tait received the ball deep inside his own half. The centre-forward began a splendid run which saw him go past five City defenders before hammering an unstoppable shot into the net from an acute angle. In the 86th minute Curry headed the equalizer to force extra-time.

Amazingly, though City went in front again when Johnstone grabbed his second goal, yet Newcastle levelled the score at 4–4 through Len White's stinging drive. And two minutes later White was back again to set the seal on United's marvellous come-back in this absorbing match. Even then City just missed claiming an equalizer themselves when Dyson hit the post in the dying seconds!

FA Cup Round 3 Replay, 9 January 1957

Manchester City: Trautmann, Leivers, Little, Barnes, Ewing, Paul, Fagan, McAdams, Johnstone, Dyson, Clarke.

City's goalscorers; Stokoe (o.g., 7), Johnstone (23, 97), Fagan (24min).

United: Simpson, Keith, Batty, Scoular, Stokoe, Casey, White, Davies, Tait, Curry, Mitchell.

United's goalscorers; Casey (47), Tait (74), Curry (86), White (102, 104).

Att: 46,990

Newcastle United 4 (1)
Nottingham Forest 3 (2)
FA Cup Round 6
9 March 1974, at St James' Park

Newcastle United have taken part in many controversial cup-ties during their history, and their 1974 sixth-round clash with Nottingham Forest was debated up and down the country for weeks afterwards. Due to a pitch invasion and subsequent protests, the FA even annulled the match and wiped the result from the record book. Nevertheless, the game remains one of the most exciting witnessed on Tyneside.

Forest were aiming for promotion in Division Two, while United were climbing up the Division One table. But despite the difference in status between the teams, it was Forest who led at half-time. Ian Bowyer gave Forest the lead in the opening minutes, then David Craig equalized from a corner-kick scramble. Nottingham were by far the better side at this point in the game and it was no surprise when Liam O'Kane

FA Cup Round 6, 9 March 1974

United: McFaul, Craig (Kennedy), Clark, McDermott, Howard, Moncur, Barrowclough, Smith, Macdonald, Tudor, Hibbitt.

United's goalscorers:
Craig (25), McDermott (68), Tudor (71), Moncur (89).

Nottingham Forest: Barron, O'Kane, Winfield, Chapman, Serella, Robertson, McKenzie, Lyall, Martin, O'Neill, Bowyer.

Forest's goalscorers:
Bowyer (2), O'Kane (41), Lyall (55).

Att: 54,500

Bobby Moncur (centre) takes the ball past Duncan McKenzie (right) in the replayed 1974 tie.

drove home a 20-yarder to restore their advantage.

In the second half it seemed the Trent club had finished United off when they were awarded a spot-kick after Craig felled Duncan McKenzie. The penalty was hotly debated and United's centre-half Pat Howard was sent off for arguing with the referee. Up stepped Lyall to hit the back of the net and Forest were 3–1 ahead.

The penalty decision and Howard's dismissal incensed the home crowd. Some fans invaded the pitch, and referee Gordon Kew led the players off for eight minutes while the police restored calm. Then, incredibly, 10-man United pulled themselves back into the tie after the stoppage. In the 68th minute Forest 'keeper Jim Barron pushed Malcolm Macdonald, and Terry McDermott stroked home the penalty. Three minutes later, with the crowd charged to boiling point, John Tudor met Hibbitt's low cross with a fabulous diving header. United were level at 3–3!

And in the final minute, Newcastle attacked again. Tudor delivered a hard cross; Macdonald nodded the ball into the path of Bobby Moncur, who volleyed the ball into the top of the net to give United a semi-final place – or so everyone thought at the time. A few days later, the FA agreed with Forest that the pitch invasion had turned the course of the game. The upshot was that United and Forest ended up with two matches at Goodison Park, but Newcastle still made their semi-final appointment, winning 1–0 after a 0–0 draw.

The Premiership Stars

Every fan has a favourite, and here we present 22 of the best and most popular Newcastle players from the club's first five years in the Premiership.

John **Barnes**

When John Barnes was granted a free transfer after 10 fabulous years in the red shirt of Liverpool, many of the Premiership's clubs immediately took an interest in the former England midfielder. Even at 34 years of age, Barnes still has much to offer, and Kenny Dalglish – the manager who signed him as a star in the making for Liverpool back in 1987 – stepped in to bring him to St James' Park in August 1997.

Born in Jamaica, Barnes made rapid progress after helping Watford to an FA Youth Cup win in 1982. He became a richly-talented winger-cum-striker in

Graham Taylor's successful line-up at Vicarage Road, reaching the 1984 FA Cup Final and England Under-21 set-up. He was soon giving eye-catching performances as a potential match-winner with the rare ability to run at defenders and deliver a telling pass or

John BARNES	
Born:	7 November 1963, Kingston, Jamaica
Position:	Midfield
Height/weight:	5ft 11in/12st 7lb
Former clubs:	Watford, Liverpool
League & Cup appearances:	0
League & Cup goals:	0
International caps:	79 (England)

John Barnes swapped Anfield for St James' Park.

shot. Dalglish was impressed, and purchased his exciting talent for £900,000 in June 1987.

At once the immensely gifted forward helped the Merseyside club to the League Championship and to a succession of trophies in the next decade. He became a key figure in the Liverpool side and twice won the Footballer of the Year Award, in 1988 and 1990. By then he was a regular for his country – capped when only 19 years of age – and will always be remembered for a quite stunning goal against Brazil in the Maracana stadium during 1984.

Barnes totalled almost 500 senior games for Liverpool and was always capable of finding the net with explosive shooting or dazzling runs. Developing into a midfield maestro of the highest quality, his vast experience will give Newcastle's midfield squad a powerful look and manager Kenny Dalglish several options to choose from.

Warren **Barton**

Warren Barton became Newcastle's most expensive purchase and Britain's costliest defender when he moved to Tyneside in June 1995 for £4 million. However, the Londoner didn't have to worry about the tag for long, as the club record was shattered a matter of days later when Les Ferdinand arrived in town.

Frank Clark, the former Newcastle favourite, had been in charge of Orient when the club rejected Barton, but Warren soon attracted the attention of big clubs while turning out for Football League newcomers Maidstone following a period in non-League soccer. The Magpies in fact tried to sign him during 1990, but wouldn't pay the £300,000 asking price. Wimbledon did – and Newcastle regretted their decision five years later!

Confident on the ball, like all of Newcastle's Premiership stars, Warren is one of several all-rounders who can play in defence or in midfield. He loves to get forward where his blond head can cause

Warren BARTON

Born:
19 March 1969, London
Position:
Full-back or Midfield
Height/weight:
5ft 11in/12st
Former clubs:
Leyton Orient, Maidstone United, Wimbledon
League & Cup appearances:
65
League & Cup goals:
2
International caps:
3 (England)

Warren Barton cost Newcastle £4m in June 1995 when United signed him from Wimbledon.

trouble in and around the opposition's penalty area. After a good start on Tyneside in the right-back role, Barton's form dipped as the pressure mounted during the 1995–96 title race. He lost his place and was on the fringe of the side until Kenny Dalglish took over from Kevin Keegan and restored the Londoner's confidence and his place in the side.

During his time in South London at Selhurst Park, he was picked by England at both "B" and full level. His debut for his country, however, lasted barely half an hour – the international fixture in Dublin during 1995 was abandoned due to a riot. Warren trained with both Arsenal and Watford as a kid and worked for an accountancy firm in the City before turning to football.

The competitive instincts of David Batty (right) have made him a favourite with Newcastle supporters.

David **Batty**

David BATTY
Born:
2 December 1968, Leeds
Position:
Midfield
Height/weight:
5ft 7in/12st 0lb
Former clubs:
Leeds United, Blackburn Rovers
League & Cup appearances:
55
League & Cup goals:
2
International caps:
25 (England)

When David Batty's career became entangled in controversy at Blackburn Rovers, following a long injury lay-off, Newcastle were alerted and the gritty Yorkshireman joined the Magpies to give them added bite in midfield.

The £3.5 million deal in February 1996 proved another good transfer purchase by Newcastle's management. Batty immediately slipped into a central anchor role and was an instant hit, both with the fans and with England, David being recalled to the national squad.

Possessing battling instincts, a cool head and immaculate distribution of the ball, Batty had been skipper of the Leeds youth side. In the first team at Elland Road by the time he was 18 years old, David went on to appear in more than 250 games for his home-town side. Quickly becoming a big personality with the Yorkshire giants, he helped Leeds to gain first promotion and then the Football League title in 1991–92, just before the Premiership arrived on the scene.

However, he was controversially sold to Blackburn in October 1993 for £2.75 million, and only an ankle injury robbed Batty of playing a major part in a second championship triumph in 1995, alongside Alan Shearer. Involved with Newcastle United in further title races in both 1996 and 1997, David is a key figure in Kenny Dalglish's plans and will undoubtedly be involved in yet another chase for silverware with the Magpies.

Peter the Great – a Tyneside hero: Peter Beardsley scored over 100 goals for United in two spells.

Peter **Beardsley**

Peter BEARDSLEY
Born: 18 January 1961, Newcastle upon Tyne
Position: Midfield/Striker
Height/weight: 5ft 8in/11st 7lb
Former clubs: Carlisle United, Vancouver Whitecaps, Manchester United (loan), Newcastle United, Liverpool, Everton
League & Cup appearances: 324
League & Cup goals: 119
International caps: 59 (England)

To many modern generation United fans, Peter Beardsley is recognized as the best and most consistent player to have pulled on the Magpie shirt.

Although Peter spent a many of his most productive years playing with Liverpool and Everton, he never lost the old passion for his local club. Beardsley is a brilliant little player who, operating just behind the front strikers, has proved devastating at both creating and scoring goals, netting over 100 for United and almost 250 in his career.

With lovely ball skills and the vision of a master playmaker, Beardsley has the enthusiasm to work and run for 90 minutes and, above all, the knack of striking absolute gems that find the net – time and time again. Peter was in fact on United's books three times: as a teenager, he was released by Bill McGarry and picked up by Carlisle where he made a name for himself in the rough and tumble of Division Three football.

After creating a big impression in North America and spending five months with Manchester United, Peter headed back to St James' Park to become Kevin Keegan's partner as the Magpies won promotion with splendour during 1984. He quickly matured and became a regular in the England set-up before transferring to Liverpool in search of trophies during July 1987. The fee was a record £1.9 million.

Championship and cup medals came his way at Anfield before he moved across Stanley Park to join Everton in 1991, becoming a firm favourite with the crowd. In a surprise move, Newcastle boss Kevin Keegan brought Peter back to Tyneside at 32 years' old, in July 1993, for £1.5 million. It was money well spent, as his experience and guile made a huge impact on United's rise as a Premiership force. Beardsley enjoyed a new lease of life and just missed out on skippering the Magpies to the title, before he moved to Bolton in August 1997.

Nicknamed Pedro, he was awarded the MBE for his services to football in 1995.

John **Beresford**

Since John Beresford made the long trip from Portsmouth to Tyneside, he has served United with distinction. One of Kevin Keegan's three key signings, alongwith Barry Venison and Paul Bracewell, for the start of the 1992–93 promotion campaign, Beresford fitted into United's style of play to perfection, being quick, attack-minded and talented on the ball.

In fact the Yorkshireman almost signed for Liverpool before settling at St James' Park, but once the Anfield deal fell through – due to a medical problem – the Magpies stepped in, and neither club or player has regretted the move since. It was with Barnsley that John became a first-team regular, having been shown the door at Maine Road by Billy McNeill. Pompey took him south, and following almost 100 games for the Fratton Park club including a noted run to the FA Cup semi-final – in which Beresford missed a penalty in a shoot-out – he was in demand by top clubs.

A former England youth captain, John is a gutsy defender with a cultured left foot and was included in both Terry Venables's and Graham Taylor's England squads. On the fringe of a full cap, he got as close as the England substitutes' bench in 1995 but unluckily wasn't called upon to appear in a white shirt.

Born into a footballing family (his father played for Chesterfield and Notts County), John battled with Robbie Elliott for the left-back role, only for Stuart Pearce to arrive at United to take the regular position.

But in Kenny Dalglish's formation, John has claimed a place as a wing-back and, in the process, often found himself in attacking positions and planting the ball in the back of the net.

John BERESFORD
Born: 4 September 1966, Sheffield
Position: Left-back
Height/weight: 5ft 6in/10st 12lb
Former clubs: Manchester City, Barnsley, Portsmouth
League & Cup appearances: 198
League & Cup goals: 2
International caps: 2 (England "B")

One of Kevin Keegan's first signings, John Beresford has been a consistent player for the Magpies since they joined the Premier League in 1993. In his new wing-back role under Kenny Dalglish, he has even got on the scoresheet.

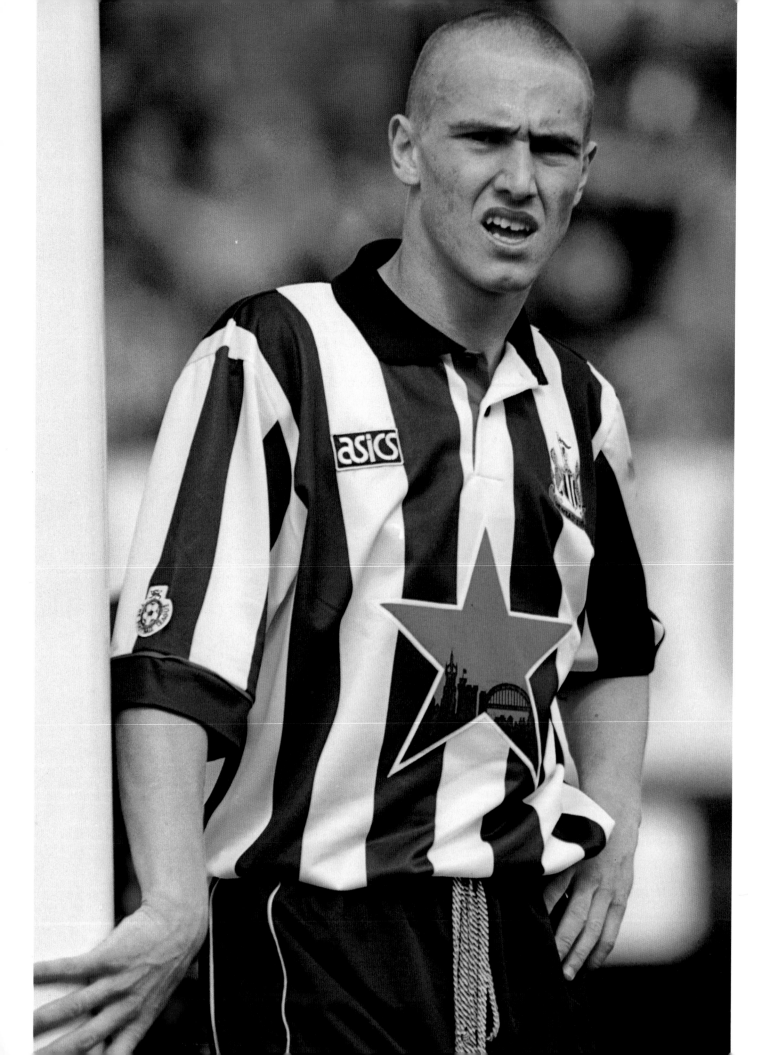

Lee **Clark**

A regular England player at schools, youth and Under-21 level – and now on the fringe of a full cap, being promoted into Glenn Hoddle's squad in the summer of 1997 – Lee Clark had been associated with the Magpies since school. His transfer to local rivals Sunderland in June 1997 in a £2.5 million deal ended a love affair between the player and the Magpies that had prospered for almost 10 years.

Following in the footsteps of local heroes Peter Beardsley, Chris Waddle and Paul Gascoigne, and first given his chance in Newcastle's side under Ossie Ardiles back in 1990, Lee was soon recognized as a star of the future.

Easy to spot with close-cropped hair, at times even completely shaven, Lee was an ever-present and key performer in the club's promotion to the Premiership in 1993, playing an attacking role from midfield. Blessed with excellent vision and the ability to knock accurate long and short passes, Clark became frustrated at not getting a regular place in Keegan's Premiership side.

Despite his huge rapport with his fellow-Geordie fans Clark was on the bench, then out injured for a period with a broken foot, and afterwards in and out of the line-up until Kenny Dalglish took over. Given a role for a while under Newcastle's new boss, Clark was again sidelined and made the reluctant decision to move on as the only way of finding a secure place. Not really wishing to leave his native North-East, Lee chose Sunderland and their new stadium on Wearside, despite the Reds' relegation into Division One. His previous link with Paul Bracewell on Tyneside was a vital ingredient in Clark's decision to drop down a division.

Lee CLARK	
Born:	27 October 1972, Wallsend
Position:	Midfield
Height/weight:	5ft 7in/11st 7lb
Former clubs:	None
League & Cup appearances:	236
League & Cup goals:	26
International caps:	11 (England Under 21)

Left: Shaven-headed Lee Clark became a big crowd favourite with his fellow Geordies.
Right: Andy Cole set a new club goalscoring record in 1993–94 – Newcastle's first season in the Premiership. Included in his 41 goals (in 45 games) was a hat-trick against Liverpool in November 1993.

Andy **Cole**

Andy Cole was purchased for a club record fee of £1.75 million from Bristol City in March 1993 as an almost unknown centre-forward who had lots of potential. He was a graduate of the FA School of Excellence at Lilleshall and a member of his country's Under-21 side. But Cole had not yet completed a full season in regular first-team action and many in the game gasped at the size of his fee.

Yet Newcastle boss Kevin Keegan saw something special in Cole: he was lightning-fast and lethal at snapping up chances in the box. And, from the first day he pulled on a black-and-white shirt, Cole repaid his manager's faith in his ability. He dominated the headlines during his short but very productive stay at St James' Park. Goals flowed in abundance as Keegan's tactics suited Cole's talents to perfection.

He helped in the latter weeks of the 1993 Division One championship victory, then took the Premiership by storm. In the 1993–94 season he was the nation's top hot-shot. Paired with Peter Beardsley, who had a huge impact on Cole's development, Andy ravaged every defence that year to net a new club record of 41 goals in only 45 games. Cole earned the PFA's Young Player of the Year award at the end of that season.

Not particularly well-built to lead the attack, Andy became a cult figure with Newcastle's supporters and in the great tradition of the Magpies' centre-forward heroes. Just when his raw talent was being steadily refined and he seemed destined for the England side, Keegan rocked the football world – and stunned every Newcastle supporter – by selling his star to Manchester United for what was then a huge fee of £7 million in January 1995.

Cole left Tyneside just as quickly as he had arrived. At Old Trafford he won his England cap, but was rarely the same scintillating player he had been wearing the Magpie colours. Out for a long period with serious injury, Cole still did a good job for the Reds.

Andy COLE

Born:
15 October 1971, Nottingham
Position:
Centre-forward
Height/weight:
5ft 11in/11st 2lb
Former clubs:
Arsenal, Fulham (loan), Bristol City
League & Cup appearances: 84
League & Cup goals: 68
International caps: 2 (England)

Les **Ferdinand**

Prior to becoming United's then record signing for a fee of £6 million in June 1995, Les Ferdinand had been one of the outstanding strikers in the country. Tall, strong and powerful, he led the attack with genuine menace, especially in the air, and Ferdinand continued in the same manner in a Magpies shirt for two seasons.

Something of a late developer in the first-class game, Les appeared on the capital's non-League scene, reaching the FA Vase final in 1986 before being picked up by QPR. However, it was not until he had been on loan to Turkish club Besiktas that Ferdinand was introduced on a regular basis at Loftus Road. He made a big impact in Instanbul, netting 21 goals in 33 games, including the winning strike in the Turkish cup final. It was a foretaste of a splendid strike-rate over the coming seasons.

Scoring 90 goals for Rangers and reaching the England side – netting on his debut against San Marino – Ferdinand became Newcastle's main target once Kevin Keegan had sold Andy Cole to Manchester United. The Magpies tracked him for many months before landing his signature, and at once the 28-year-old Londoner took on the mantle of the new Number Nine hero. Ferdinand was an instant hit and lifted the PFA Player of the Year trophy in 1996, the first Newcastle United player to do so. The Toon Army loved his power-play, and even when paired with Alan Shearer, Ferdinand earned respect for handing the famous centre-forward's shirt to the local lad and taking the Number 10 jersey himself.

The partnership of Shearer and Ferdinand was the best in the business for a season before a bid of £6 million from Tottenham was too good an offer for United to refuse in July 1997. Newcastle cashed in on a player who had served them well, but who was now 30 years of age.

His cousin, Rio, appears for West Ham United in defence – and looks destined to join Les in the England set-up too.

Les FERDINAND

Born:
8 December 1966, London
Position:
Striker
Height/weight:
5ft 11in/13st 5lb
Former clubs:
Queens Park Rangers, Brentford (loan), Besiktas (Tur) (loan)
League & Cup appearances: 83
League & Cup goals: 50
International caps: 13 (England)

Although only at St James' Park for two seasons, Les Ferdinand became hugely popular with the fans.

Ruel **Fox**

Ruel FOX

Born:
14 January 1968, Ipswich
Position:
Outside-right or Midfield
Height/weight:
5ft 6in/10st
Former clubs:
Ipswich Town, Norwich City
League & Cup appearances: 70
League & Cup goals: 14
International caps:
2 (England B)

Ruel Fox became the first of United's Premiership multi-million pound men when Kevin Keegan paid out £2.25 million to bring him to Tyneside in February 1994 to help reinforce their position in the elite division. Compact and tricky, Fox showed he could be a handful for any defence, rising to prominence in more than 200 games for an entertaining Norwich line-up that impressed many, including fine performances in the UEFA Cup.

Ruel was an immediate hit with Newcastle's supporters. He showed delightful touches on the ball and linked with Andy Cole with menace during the 1993–94 and 1994–95 seasons. His form was good enough to earn recognition for England, Fox winning England "B" honours. He could also be relied upon to grab a few goals, and was especially dangerous when cutting in from the wing to hit a shot at goal.

However, despite his popularity, the arrival of David Ginola in Kevin Keegan's more international squad for the start of the 1995–96 season saw a change in team formation to accomodate the big Frenchman. With Ginola and Gillespie being handed the wide berths, Fox found himself sitting on the bench more often than having a starting role in games.

In search of regular first-team action, Ruel moved to Tottenham in October 1995, Newcastle receiving almost double the fee they had paid for to get him: Spurs had to shell out £4 million to take the winger to White Hart Lane.

Left: Ruel Fox, a tricky player either on the wing or in midfield.

Keith GILLESPIE

Born:
18 February 1975, Larne
Position:
Outside-right
Height/weight:
5ft 10in/11st 5lb
Former clubs:
Manchester United, Wigan Athletic (loan)
League & Cup appearances: 95
League & Cup goals: 10
International caps:
17 (Northern Ireland)

Keith Gillespie arrived as part of the Andy Cole deal in 1995 and he is now a regular for both Newcastle and Northern Ireland.

Keith **Gillespie**

Keith Gillespie arrived on Tyneside as part of the multi-million pound deal that sent Andy Cole to Old Trafford in January 1995, and quickly showed the football world that he was no make-weight in the headline transfer. The young Northern Ireland winger proved he could become a huge personality himself, being fast and direct with a cutting edge which would make him a matchwinner on the right touchline.

Gillespie had made a big impression on Newcastle's manager Kevin Keegan in a series of matches against the Magpies before that Cole deal. Already an international, despite his youth, Keith

Above: The Republic of Ireland's first-choice 'keeper, Shay Given, was with Kenny Dalglish at Blackburn. Right: Bradford born and bred, Des Hamilton has left Bradford City and is trying to break in at Newcastle.

became a regular in United's line-up and showed balance and control of the ball as well as searing pace running at defenders. And when he teamed up with David Ginola on Newcastle's opposite flank, the Magpies' attacking wing play became a feature of the Premiership.

The contrast of Ginola's tricky skills on the left touchline, to Gillespie's more direct approach on the right, reminded many older supporters of a similar wing duo from Newcastle team of the 1950s: Bobby Mitchell and Tommy Walker, who helped the Magpies to FA Cup successes.

A former FA Youth Cup-winner with Manchester United in 1992 and 1993, Keith had been connected with Alex Ferguson's excellent junior set-up since he was 14. Playing for his country at every level and gaining his full cap when only 19, Gillespie is now a regular in international football with Northern Ireland. Before joining the Magpies he earned some experience during a loan period at Wigan.

With plenty of years ahead of him, Gillespie has now learned the basics of the the game at the highest level. The next stage in his footballing development – to establish himself as one of the Premiership's really big stars – is squarely in his sights.

Shay **Given**

Of Irish birth, Shay Given is one of several promising young players signed by Kenny Daglish during the close season of 1997. Destined to become a big star in the coming years, Given is tipped to serve the Republic of Ireland as first-choice goalkeeper for the next decade. Although reserve to Tim Flowers at Ewood Park, Given was rated very highly and proved his worth every time he was handed an opportunity.

That was especially the case when he was loaned out to Swindon and Sunderland. At Roker Park the youngster performed well during the 1995–96 season and kept 12 clean sheets in his 17 outings. Confident and agile, he is assured at collecting the cross-ball

Shay GIVEN

Born:
20 April 1976, Lifford
Position:
Goalkeeper
Height/weight:
6ft 1in/12st 10lb
Former clubs:
Celtic, Blackburn Rovers, Swindon Town (loan), Sunderland (loan)
League & Cup appearances: 0
League & Cup goals:
0
International caps:
10 (Republic of Ireland)

and has brilliant shot-stopping ability.

Given joined Celtic as a teenager and was coached initially by former United midfielder Mick Martin when he was assistant to Liam Brady at Parkhead. Shay was taken to Lancashire by Kenny Dalglish and it was no surprise when United's boss revived the partnership with Given during the summer – a deal which was settled by tribunal at £1.5 million after Newcastle tested the Bosman ruling in the UK against Blackburn's valuation of £2 million.

Having also had a brief period at Old Trafford as a youngster, Given will be out to show he can claim the United goalkeeper's shirt and repay the faith shown in him by his manager.

Des **Hamilton**

Yorkshire born and bred, Des Hamilton was Kenny Dalglish's first purchase as Newcastle manager. Versatile enough to operate either as an orthodox full-back, a more modern wing-back, or in midfield, Des cost the Magpies £1.375 million when he signed towards the end of the 1996–97 season.

His rise to fame was quite astonishing. Almost unknown to supporters outside his home town of Bradford, Hamilton made his surprise big-money move to Tyneside. Within a matter of days he was rubbing shoulders with some of the Premiership's biggest names and was then called up to the England Under-21 squad, eventually gaining his first cap against Poland.

Hamilton began his footballing career at the Pulse Stadium in Bradford as a trainee and made his senior debut in the game during May 1994 when he scored in a 2–1 victory over Barnet. Des – real name Derrick – had a taste of that special Wembley experience when Bradford reached the Play-off finals in 1996. Hamilton was on the scoresheet on that memorable day as City were promoted following a 2–0 victory.

Athletic and fast, he also appeared for the Football League representative side. United's investment in the youngster should prove sound over the coming years.

Des HAMILTON	
Born:	15 August 1976, Bradford
Position:	Full-back or Midfield
Height/weight:	5ft 10in/12st 13lb
Former clubs:	Bradford City
League & Cup appearances:	0
League & Cup goals:	0
International caps:	1 (England Under 21)

Shaka **Hislop**

One of several Londoners to have served the Magpies well during their Premiership years, Shaka Hislop had been a target of Kevin Keegan for several months before the 6ft 4ins goalkeeper arrived at St James' Park. Many judges considered Hislop the best guardian outside the Premier League, and his performances for Reading showed he was agile and good in the air. Newcastle paid out £1.575 million when he joined the Magpies in August 1995.

Although born in the capital of Caribbean parents – he was named "Shaka" after a Zulu king – he spent most of his youth in Trinidad, where his father worked as a lawyer and magistrate. Playing teenage football and cricket alongside Brian Lara and Dwight Yorke of Aston Villa, Shaka later moved to the USA where he studied at an American university. Awarded a four-year footballing scholarship in the States, he was spotted by Reading's ex-Magpie boss Mark McGhee while playing in a friendly for Baltimore Blast against Aston Villa. A stunning display earned him a crack at top professional football.

Hislop rapidly became first choice at Elm Park, making 126 appearances for the Biscuitmen, helping Reading to promotion in 1994 and very nearly into the Premiership, losing a Wembley Play-off a year later.

One of United's tallest-ever players, along with Dave Beasant and George Reilly, Shaka wears size 11 boots and size 11 gloves! He has rivalled the popular Pavel Srnicek for his first season at St James' Park and now has Shay Given as well to battle against for the Number One spot.

Shaka played for the Trinidad schools and youth international sides, while his brother Kona had a spell on United's books before continuing his football career in local North-East leagues.

Shaka HISLOP	
Born:	22 February 1969, London
Position:	Goalkeeper
Height:	6ft 4in/14st 4lb
Former clubs:	Reading
League & Cup appearances:	50
League & Cup goals:	0
International caps:	None

Right: Shaka Hislop, one of United's tallest ever players, rivals Pavel Srnicek and Shay Given for the first-choice goalkeeper's position.

Steve **Howey**

Beginning his career as an out-and-out striker in more than 30 games for the Magpies, beginning with his debut against Manchester United in May 1989, Steve Howey's progress in that role had been destined to end up in the lower divisions. But a crucial switch into the heart of the back four was made in 1991, initially by Ossie Ardiles, but more positively by Kevin Keegan therafter, and Howey's career took off.

Installed in the pivotal role for the 1992–93 championship campaign, Steve showed that his height and build, as well as his pace, aggression and passing ability, were perfect qualities for the position. His ability to move forward and distribute accurately fitted neatly into United's style; and as a bonus, Steve is always dangerous in attack where his original striker's instincts give United's attack a boost from set-pieces.

Overcoming a troublesome groin injury which saw the Wearsider out of action following several operations, Howey became a regular in Terry Venables's England squad – this after being selected numerous times for the Under 21 line-up but having to withdraw due to injury. It was another unlucky mishap during England's preparations for the Euro '96 championship that kept him on the sidelines, and then Steve was back on the operating table after a niggling calf injury failed to clear up during the 1996–97 campaign.

Now fit again, Howey (whose brother Lee played for Sunderland) will be striving to reclaim both his Magpie and England places.

Steve HOWEY

Born:
26 October 1971, Sunderland
Position:
Centre-half
Height/weight:
6ft 2in/11st 12lb
Former clubs:
None
League & Cup appearances: 186
League & Cup goals:
7 goals
International caps:
4 (England)

Left: Although born in Sunderland, Steve Howey has made his name in United's black and white shirt. After starting out as a striker, he has won England caps as a defender.
Right: General Lee – United's midfield master, Rob Lee. Since joining the Magpies in 1992 from Charlton Athletic, Rob has become a key figure in the rise and rise of Newcastle United.

Robert **Lee**

After appearing on more than 300 occasions for Charlton Athletic, in which he netted more than 60 goals and was rated one of the best players outside the top division, Robert Lee made the journey north and very quickly became one of the best performers in the Premiership too. Joining United for £700,000 in September 1992, he played an important role on the wing as Newcastle won the first division championship that season.

Very strong in possession, able to hold off challenges on the ball, Lee switched to a more conventional midfield role as United started life in the Premier League. Full of energy, his work-rate is high and Rob is always able to hit stinging shots or ghost into the penalty box and score goals. Lee was elevated to the England squad and scored on his debut for his country against Romania. According to his then manager, Kevin Keegan, he was the best all-round midfield player in the country.

The cornerstone of United's midfield during their Premiership life, Rob Lee scored a marvellous hat-trick in the UEFA Cup against Antwerp, the first Magpie player to do so. One of his goals in that tie in Belgium is also the quickest on record in a European fixture for the Magpies, netted after only 50 seconds.

Appointed club captain in succession to Peter Beardsley, the Londoner is one of Glenn Hoddle's midfield squad and he will be hoping to be selected for the World Cup finals, if England qualify.

Perhaps the biggest compliment to have come his way is that there are many football judges who believe that if Robert Lee is playing well, then Newcastle is playing well too.

Brought up in London's East End before turning pro with Charlton, Rob worked as a shipping clerk and was a turnstile operator at The Valley. He began his adult football career with Essex non-League club Hornchurch after Spurs (for being too slight) and West Ham (when still a teenager) had both rejected him.

Robert LEE

Born:
1 February 1966, London
Position:
Midfield
Height/weight:
5ft 11in/11st 13lb
Former clubs:
Charlton Athletic
League & Cup appearances: 219
League & Cup goals: 50
International caps:
13 (England)

Darren **Peacock**

Darren Peacock became the country's most expensive defender at the time he joined the Magpies from Queens Park Rangers in March 1994. With a £2.7 million fee exchanged, Peacock had something to prove and it took a while for the long-haired (and pony-tailed) centre-half to settle at St James' Park. But for the 1995–96 and 1996–97 seasons, he displayed enough grit and determination in his performances to make him United's Player of the Season in many supporters' eyes – and all this despite unjustified criticism from elsewhere in the country.

Peacock became a crowd favourite on Tyneside, a far cry from his early days in the game. Rejected by both Bristol City and Rovers, he found himself with struggling Welsh club Newport County, who were on their way out of the league. Apart from having to cope with a broken leg which needed a bone graft, Darren saw the club struggle for cash and grant virtually the whole staff free transfers, including himself. But he picked up his career with Hereford and established himself as a commanding defender in the lower divisions.

His move to QPR in December 1990 gave Darren a higher platform and he developed further in London, making almost 150 appearances for the club. Kevin Keegan liked what he saw at Rangers and was persistent in his chase to bring the defender to the club. Although Darren hasn't represented his country, he has certainly held his own alongside many colleagues of international pedigree.

Darren's only club honour so far is a 1990 Welsh Cup winner's medal. He is hoping for something more prestigious with United in the next couple of seasons.

Darren PEACOCK

Born:
3 February 1968, Bristol
Position:
Centre-half
Height/weight:
6ft 2in/12st 12lb
Former clubs:
Bristol City, Bristol Rovers, Newport County, Hereford United, Queens Park Rangers
League & Cup appearances: 146
League & Cup goals: 4
International caps:
None

Right: Big Darren Peacock has given plenty of very determined performances for the Magpies. After toiling in the lower divisions, the Bristol-born central defender has commanded respect from the Toon Army ranks.

Stuart Pearce joined United from Forest and immediately made a big impression in Newcastle's defence.

Stuart **Pearce**

Although Stuart Pearce could be called one of the veterans of the Premiership, the powerful defender has plenty to offer the Magpies. Superbly fit and as enthusiastic as any of his younger team-mates, Pearce was signed by Kenny Dalglish after Nottingham Forest had been relegated. He arrived on Tyneside on a free transfer and was an astute signing by the Newcastle management.

Newcastle acquired a highly experienced full-back with an intelligent football brain, and one who is tough as they come, with an unbeatable will to win. He was just what Newcastle's defence needed: a commanding and inspiring influence on the field. And Pearce still has the ability to pull on an England shirt too. He will be striving to add to his already formidable total of over 70 caps for his country this season despite his age. Solidly built, the Londoner has already appeared in World Cup finals for England and Stuart will be aiming to be in France alongside many of his United colleagues next summer.

With Nottingham Forest since 1985, Pearce had developed into something of a legend at the City Ground by the time he departed during July 1997. Skipper of Forest, he reached three Wembley finals in 1989, 1990 and 1991 and totalled over 500 League and Cup outings for the Reds as well as netting almost a century of goals – a great record for a defender. Pearce, with his dangerous crossing ability and stunning shooting, will reinforce Newcastle's already awesome attacking options.

Stuart remains a left-back of absolute quality and has quickly become as popular on Tyneside as he was alongside the Trent. There is little doubt he will become a cult figure with the Toon Army.

Stuart PEARCE
Born: 24 April 1962, London
Position: Left-back
Height/weight: 5ft 10in/12st 12lb
Former clubs: Coventry City, Nottingham Forest
League & Cup appearances: 0
League & Cup goals: 0
International caps: 76 (England)

Ian **Rush**

When Alan Shearer unluckily injured his ankle on the eve of the new 1997–98 season, Newcastle found themselves with a striking problem to solve. The departure of Les Ferdinand to Tottenham had created a void and Kenny Dalglish turned to his former colleague at Liverpool, Ian Rush. Then with Leeds, the Welsh international and Anfield goalscoring phenomenon joined the St James' Park staff on a free transfer.

Although 36 years of age, Rush is still a striker to be reckoned with. His record proves that he has all the know-how to fill Alan Shearer's shirt. In 15 seasons with Liverpool Ian crashed home 229 League goals in 469 outings. He topped the 300-goal mark in all games for the Reds and was the most dangerous striker

Goal master Ian Rush was a Liverpool legend, but he is now wearing the black and white stripes.

With a sweet left foot, Scott Sellars did much to consolidate Newcastle's position in the Premiership.

Ian RUSH

Born:
20 October 1961,
St Asaph
Position:
Striker
Height/weight:
6ft 0in/12st 6 lb
Former clubs:
Chester City, Liverpool,
Juventus, Leeds United
**League & Cup
appearances:** 0
League & Cup goals:
0
International caps:
73 (Wales)

around during the Eighties and much of the Nineties.

Starting his career at Chester, he was picked up by Bob Paisley as an 18-year-old and grabbed a place in the Liverpool side during 1981–82, ending up with 30 goals. From that year Rush, like Barnes and his managerial duo of Dalglish and McDermott, picked up trophy after trophy for Liverpool, including the European Champions' Cup in 1984. Rush was both Footballer of the Year and Player of the Year in that successful season.

With positional awareness, speed and a high work-rate, Rush was a deadly striker in the box. He had a brief spell in Italy with Juventus during 1987–88, but returned to Merseyside to continue his goals haul. A

regular for Wales, no other player has scored more than the 28 goals he netted for his country.

Holder of the post-war goalscoring record for FA Cup football, Rush will fill the Newcastle centre-forward role and hold the respect of every professional and supporter in the country.

Scott Sellars

Scott Sellars arrived on Tyneside as a replacement for the aging Kevin Sheedy during Newcastle's run-in to their successful promotion campaign in the 1992–93 season. With a left foot just as sweet as the former Everton midfielder's, Sellars arrived at Gallowgate in March 1993 for a £600,000 fee having seen no regular first-team action for a year, being unable to break into the Leeds line-up.

With the Elland Road club in a second spell following a successful stint at Blackburn, where he won promotion under Kenny Dalglish after four Play-offs, the England Under-21 player failed to settle at Leeds

Scott SELLARS

Born:
27 November 1965,
Sheffield
Position:
Midfield
Height/weight:
5ft 7in/9st 10lb
Former clubs:
Leeds United, Blackburn
Rovers
**League & Cup
appearances:** 75
League & Cup goals:
8
International caps:
3 (England Under-21)

and was more than happy to slip into Kevin Keegan's left-midfield role. He showed the Geordie crowd that with his delicate ball skills and astute use of the ball he was to be a key player in the Magpies' team plan. A free kick expert, during the early part of his career he was chased by Manchester United but ended up with Leeds, making his debut as a 17-year-old.

He helped to give the Magpies balance on the left, and as he entered the Premiership with Newcastle, Sellars was regarded as an unsung hero of United's star-studded combination. He was accurate with his passing and always a danger at pulling the ball back, especially for Andy Cole. But Scott was in the treatment room for a long lay-off with a cartilage injury, and by the time he was fit again the presence of David Ginola made sure he was destined to spend most of his time on the bench.

Sellars moved to Bolton in December 1995, where the Yorkshireman helped Wanderers back into the Premier League in 1997.

Alan **Shearer**

The world-record £15 million purchase of England striker Alan Shearer during the summer of 1996 was a dramatic homecoming for the Tynesider who had always supported the Black-and-Whites. Once at St James' Park for trials as a teenager, Alan ended up at The Dell and developed quickly on the South Coast. He netted a hat-trick on his first full League outing for the Saints – at 17, the youngest player to do so in the top flight. And by the time he had scored 13 goals for the England Under-21 side in only 11 games, Shearer was in demand.

Kevin Keegan tried, and failed, to bring him to Gallowgate in 1992, and it was Kenny Dalglish who secured his signature for £3.6 million in July 1992. At the time that deal was a huge sum, but in the next four seasons Alan became the Premier League's most dev-

astating striker and the fee was judged a bargain.

Perhaps the ultimate all-round leader of the attack, Alan is strong, aggressive and intelligent, possessing power in both feet. Clinical in the box and spectacular from long range, with a searing turn of pace and simply outstanding in the air, Blackburn reaped the reward through his goals; 130 all told for Rovers, almost a goal a game over four seasons. He was very much the key to the Ewood club lifting the title in 1995.

Top scorer in the hugely successful Euro '96 championships and now skipper of his country, Alan stands alongside Brazilian Ronaldo as the world's best striker. He

Alan SHEARER

Born:
13 August 1970,
Newcastle upon Tyne
Position:
Centre-forward
Height/weight:
6ft/12st 6lb
Former clubs:
Southampton, Blackburn
Rovers
**League & Cup
appearances:** 39
League & Cup goals:
28
International caps:
35 (England)

Shear magic – A local lad made good, Alan Shearer is the Geordies' number one favourite.

has taken to the famous Newcastle United Number Nine shirt as everyone knew he would, wearing the stripes with the pride and passion of a Geordie brought up on the terraces of St James' Park.

Shearer has twice won the PFA Player of the Year award, in 1995 and 1997, and was also voted the FWA Footballer of the Year in 1994. Reunited with Kenny Dalglish on Tyneside, Alan was unlucky to be sidelined with a bad ankle injury just as the new 1997–98 season was about to start. But once he regains his fitness, England's centre-forward will lead Newcastle's push for honours.

Barry Venison

A product of Sunderland's juniors, Barry Venison was a teenage star at Roker Park and made 206 appearances before a big-money transfer to Liverpool in July 1986. He was the Wearsiders' captain at Wembley in the 1985 League Cup Final when 20. His maturity made sure he was quickly picked up by the country's top side.

Venison played a part in gaining championship and cup success at Anfield before returning to his native North-East during the summer of 1992 for what was at the time a bargain fee of £250,000. Venison marshalled United's defence from the right-back position as the Magpies stormed into the Premiership. Also stepping in at centre-half, he was comfortable with the ball and was totally committed, showing determination and inspirational qualities which rallied team-mates and fans alike.

A flamboyant character and a dedicated follower of fashion, Barry was an immediate favourite with the supporters, despite his earlier Sunderland connections. As the Magpies consolidated their position in the Premier League he moved to a holding role in midfield. Such was the success of that switch in position that he was capped by England. Venison – easily identified by his flowing blond hair – played the game

A dedicated follower of fashion, Barry Venison was a hero on Tyneside even though he began his career at Sunderland.

Barry VENISON	
Born:	16 August 1964, Consett
Position:	Full-back/midfield
Height/weight:	5ft 10in/12st 3lb
Former clubs:	Sunderland, Liverpool
League & Cup appearances:	130
League & Cup goals:	1
International caps:	2 (England)

on Tyneside with immense pride in the shirt he wore. During his three years with United, Barry often skippered the side.

He moved to Turkey in June 1995, teaming up with Graeme Souness at Galatasaray, but that deal never worked out and Barry was quickly back on the Premiership beat, joining Southampton during October 1995 for £850,000.

Steve **Watson**

On many occasions local lad Steve Watson has held his own in United's side of internationals. A versatile player who has been linked with the Magpies since he was a 10-year-old schoolboy, Watson has settled at right-back but can equally operate in midfield, at centre-back or even up-front. And he is also a more than adequate goalkeeper!

Tall and commanding, Steve has skill on the ball and ability to strike the net, hitting several spectacular efforts for United, including one magic moment at Anfield in a League Cup tie during 1995–96. An England Under-21 regular until he grew too old for the squad, Watson was on the fringe of a full call-up by Glenn Hoddle during 1996–97. Steve's introduction into United's first team was as a teenager, and he became the club's youngest ever player – at 16 years and 223 days – when he appeared against Wolverhampton Wanderers in 1990.

Before Watson was 20 he had clocked up almost 100 games for the Magpies and has now, in his early 20s, has passed the 200 mark. The popular local product had at times to spend a long period on the touchline, yet whenever he has been given a chance Watson has produced impressive displays in a number of roles. Energetic, with loads of enthusiasm, he also possesses a dangerous long throw, which in his younger days was executed with a somersault!

Steve also represented England at youth level and appeared in two junior World Cup tournaments.

Steve WATSON

Born:
1 April 1974, North Shields
Position:
Full-back/Utility player
Height/weight:
6ft/12st 7lb
Former clubs:
None
League & Cup appearances: 206
League & Cup goals:
13
International caps:
12 (England Under-21)

Geordie boy: Local lad Steve Watson has held his own in a team of international stars at Newcastle. One of Watson's greatest assets is that he can adapt his game to fill almost any role for the Magpies. Steve has been a regular in the England under-21 team, and will be hoping to make the step up to Glenn Hoddle's full international squad during the 1997–98 season.

The Newcastle Managers

To manage a club of Newcastle's stature and size is an immense task today. It takes a man who is at the very top of the sport.

Newcastle United, like many football clubs, did not appoint a manager for much of the period before the Second World War. And even then, the character in charge – as late as 1961, in the case of St James' Park – had little power. His decisions were constantly being overruled by the all-powerful board of directors. Only

Life on the bench: Kevin Keegan and Terry McDermott can only watch as United battle for three points.

Director and manager Stan Seymour, known throughout football as "Mr Newcastle".

in what could be called the modern era of the game, those decades from the Sixties and Seventies to the present, did "the boss" get full control.

Before the appointment of their first manager in 1930, United's team affairs were the responsibility of a directors' committee. The board were in charge of buying and selling players, picking the team and all other aspects of the club. Though they appointed a trainer, he was very much someone who put the players through their paces in terms of fitness, and not a coach as we know them today.

Football by 1930 was beginning to change slowly. At first, Newcastle followed the line that clubs should have a dedicated manager to look after the players and team. In January 1930 they appointed as manager a famous Scottish international player, Andy Cunningham, an ex-Rangers schemer who had been on Tyneside as a player for almost a year. In fact, he became the first player-boss in the top division.

Cunningham wasn't yet 40 years of age, and in managerial terms was a young and bright appoint-

ment. Early on in his reign he guided United to Wembley glory in the FA Cup of 1932, but he was also in charge when the Magpies fell from the top division for the first time ever two years later, despite having a side full of capable players.

The Scot was replaced in 1935 when a more experienced personality arrived on Tyneside in the shape of Tom Mather. Having fashioned Stoke City into a good side, taking them to promotion and introducing the likes of Stanley Matthews to the game, Mather controlled United's bid to regain their Division One place in the years leading up to the outbreak of war.

From Chorley, the well-liked Mather introduced youngsters such as Stubbins and Cairns to United's first-team shirt, while also bringing experienced England players including Birkett and Bowden to Tyneside. Newcastle did well in the 1936–37 season, just missing out on promotion, and were heading in the right direction when war was declared in September 1939.

The major competitions ceased for the duration of the hostilities, and Mather's chance of taking United into the top division had gone. By the time peace had been restored, a new man was in charge at St James' Park: but one who belonged in the boardroom.

Stan Seymour had been a fabulous player for United and was appointed to the board in 1938 to give the club a fresh impetus. Throughout the Forties and Fifties Seymour had a huge influence on playing affairs, even in periods when the club also had a team boss. Although he was a director, Seymour was manager in all but name, and carried the title of "Honorary Manager" when United lifted the FA Cup in 1951 and 1952.

Newcastle did appoint George Martin to the post in 1947, but behind the scenes Seymour was still in control. Together they led the club to promotion the following year, before the former Everton player left to take charge of Aston Villa. Seymour was then in sole charge until the end of 1954 when another respected personality arrived at Newcastle: Duggie Livingstone.

Having proved himself a first-class coach on the Continent, Livingstone brought new, modern ideas to St James' Park, most of which did not go down well with the majority of the players. And Seymour had to step in when Livingstone's 1955 FA Cup Final side was presented to the directors without the name of Jackie Milburn. Seymour exploded – and the manager's team was changed, with Milburn in the forward line.

Not surprisingly, although United lifted the trophy that year, Livingstone quickly moved on after that.

FA Cup-winning captain then boss Joe Harvey, flanked by Bobby Moncur (left) and Malcolm Macdonald.

The directors resumed total control of team matters until ex-Manchester United star Charlie Mitten arrived in 1958. Another man with a novel outlook, he was ideally placed to drag United into the modern era of football: and though he succeeded, at least in part, there were many fireworks along the way as the manager clashed with warring factions on the board. United's relegation in 1961 was the point at which Mitten departed, and Newcastle looked again for a new man.

By this time United's directors had realized they had to appoint someone who would have full control, with little interference from the top. Football was rapidly being brought up to date and there was no room for director-managers in the mould of Seymour. After the stop-gap appointment of trainer Norman Smith, the Magpies' former captain Joe Harvey arrived as boss in June 1962.

Harvey, a gritty Yorkshireman but an adopted Geordie, at once set about rebuilding the Black-and-Whites. A huge character, well-liked by players and fans alike, Harvey led United to the Division Two championship in 1965 and then began to create an entertaining side packed with star quality. He lifted the Fairs Cup in 1969 and took United to Wembley in 1974, but was denied a major domestic trophy by a troubling lack of consistency on the pitch.

In 1975 Harvey gave way to the controversial Gordon Lee, who arrived from Blackburn Rovers. Lee was a manager who believed that only hard work and total commitment brought success. That was fair enough; but he also had no time for flamboyant and talented players, hero figures such as Malcolm Macdonald, and his decision to sell Newcastle's star centre-forward to Arsenal rocked the club. Lee did take United back to Wembley in the League Cup in 1976, but then sold himself to Everton a year later and left United in deep trouble.

Then came Lee's assistant, Richard Dinnis, whose brief and stormy period in charge almost resulted in a players' strike when the board moved to replace him. Dinnis earned United a UEFA Cup place in 1977, but then his management fell apart when United became relegation candidates the following year. He was sacked: and in stepped hard man Bill McGarry, a former England player and prominent for a period in charge at Wolves.

McGarry attempted to save United, but saw the side

Above: Jack Charlton became manager in 1984.
Below: Ossie Ardiles had a torrid time in charge.

lower divisions, having been in charge at Chesterfield. When he was appointed in September 1980, United were frankly desperate for a man who could lead them back to Division One. With crowds dwindling, Newcastle's status as one of the traditionally big clubs was rapidly slipping away.

At first Cox struggled to hit on the right formula, but a masterly signing in the close season of 1982 brought Kevin Keegan into Arthur's plans – and with him a meteoric revival in the fortunes of St James' Park. Keegan's influence gave Cox the edge he needed, and the Magpies were promoted two years later. Almost immediately, however, the manager fell into dispute with United's board. He departed for Derby – and big Jack Charlton entered the action.

A Geordie hero, the strong-willed Charlton had one season in charge and consolidated the Magpies' place in the top division. But, under fire from some sections of the crowd for the style of football he preached, Jack walked out just as the 1985–86 season was about to kick off.

Newcastle were in turmoil. Coach and former goalkeeper Willie McFaul filled the breach, and for three seasons the Northern Ireland international did a sound if not spectacular job. United finished in eighth place at the end of the 1987–88 programme but, more significantly, United's fans had seen the departure of stars Waddle, Beardsley and Gascoigne. They were becoming increasingly restless.

McFaul was sacked in October 1988 and the "Bald Eagle", Jim Smith, landed in the chair with United facing another spell in Division Two. Smith began a huge buying and selling spree which resulted in the Magpies missing out on promotion by a whisker – falling in the Play-offs to local rivals Sunderland. The pressure to succeed was enormous, and during Smith's reign, political factions off the pitch started a bid to oust the much-criticized board of directors. The share-war raging in the background for control of the club did little to help Smith in his bid to gain promotion, and he eventually resigned.

Argentinian Ossie Ardiles was a big-name appointment in March 1991. The likeable former World Cup star had a difficult task at a most difficult time in the history of the club, and his brand of attractive, but defensively suspect, football sent the Magpies heading the wrong way in Division Two. Instead of moving towards the top division, they slumped towards Division Three for the first time in their history! Ardiles' reign did not last long.

tumble into Division Two, and then began the task of rebuilding the team yet again. He came close to putting a strong line-up together, signing the formidable Peter Withe in a record deal, but a sustained promotion challenge never materialized and he was dismissed in 1980.

Arthur Cox was a respected manager from the

Special K

In February 1992, Newcastle United stood in need of a saviour – someone who could rescue the club from total collapse. Chairman Sir John Hall acted swiftly and decisively to appoint Kevin Keegan, a man with the personality, charisma and knowledge to pull it off. As a player the former England captain had enjoyed huge success with Liverpool and SV Hamburg, spent two years at Southampton and ended his playing career with United. Keegan accepted the formidable challenge to save Newcastle from the drop – which would probably have meant liquidation of the club.

Joining forces with another former Newcastle, Liverpool and England star, Terry McDermott, Keegan began to act. Fans and players backed him to the hilt and Newcastle survived, securing their Division Two status – but only just. Accepting a permanent post during the summer of 1992, Keegan was to transform the Magpies in the coming years. From a struggling outfit, unattractive to watch, they became one of the superclubs, the most entertaining club in the country and with a side of international stars.

Though born near Doncaster, Keegan came from a Geordie family – his father hailed from Hetton-le-Hole, while his grandfather was a hero of the pit disaster at West Stanley – and formed a bond with Tyneside's public like no other man before. A unique relationship of hero and fan, it was the key ingredient of Newcastle's success.

At the peak of his playing career Keegan was world-class, making 63 appearances for his country and skippering England 31 times. Operating in midfield or up-front, he possessed control, awareness and the ability to create and combine with others, as well as having a deadly finish himself. Kevin had lots of courage, worked hard and ran for 90 minutes. In total, he appeared on almost 800 occasions in senior football and netted 274 goals.

With his reputation, Keegan the manager had little trouble in attracting players to Newcastle – many had been his fans as youngsters. He was given plenty of money to spend and he spent big, yet wisely. Rarely did he waste money on a player who either did not succeed in a Magpie shirt or was later sold at a loss.

Keegan fashioned a string of celebrated line-ups. After winning the Division One Championship in a style that pleased everybody, Kevin's team stormed the Premiership. Newcastle rivalled Manchester United, Liverpool and Arsenal as the division's strongest sides, but the Magpies just missed the Premier League title in 1996: Kevin was immensely disappointed at letting the trophy slip from his grasp when Newcastle were clear leaders and favourites to lift the championship.

The following season affected him for the worse. The pressure to succeed was too great, and by Christmas 1996 speculation was rife that United's high-profile manager was to depart, in readiness for the club's much-heralded flotation which required commitment from both the manager and the board. Keegan resigned in January 1997, walking out on football altogether: but despite this, he remains a hugely popular figure with Newcastle supporters.

Kevin KEEGAN

Born:
Armthorpe, near Doncaster, 1951
Playing Career:
Scunthorpe United, Liverpool, SV Hamburg (Ger), Southampton, Newcastle United.
Honours:
63 England caps, 1 unofficial England cap, 5 Under-23 caps.
League champions 1973, 1976, 1977.
League Div. 2 promotion 1984.
FA Cup winner 1974, FA Cup finalist 1977.
European Cup winner 1977, European Cup finalist 1980.
UEFA Cup-winner 1973, 1976.
Bundesliga champions 1979.
FWA Footballer of the Year 1976.
PFA Player of the Year 1982.
European Footballer of the Year 1978, 1979.
West German Footballer of the Year 1978.
Awarded the OBE in 1982.

Managerial Career:
Newcastle United.
Honours:
League champions 1993.
Managerial Record:

1992–93	Division 1	Champions	FAC R5	LC R3	
1993–94	Premier Lg	3rd	FAC R4	LC R3	
1994–95	Premier Lg	6th	FAC R6	LC R4	UEFAC R2
1995–96	Premier Lg	2nd	FAC R3	LC R5	
1996–97	Premier Lg	2nd	FAC –	LC R4	UEFAC –

A hero to a whole region, Kevin Keegan could do little wrong at St James' Park and his brand of entertaining soccer delighted millions. He built the foundations for United's modern success, putting together a squad of players to rival the very best in the Premier League.

King Kenny

The man to replace Kevin Keegan had to be someone of equal standing: Newcastle's fans would have not accepted an ordinary mortal. Kenny Dalglish was one of only a few who could have stepped into Keegan's shoes. As a player, the Scot had also been a legend for Liverpool and his country. Beginning his career with Glasgow Celtic, Dalglish had won every honour in the game north of the border over and over again, and was the star of Scottish football before his £440,000 move to Anfield – ironically to fill the place of Kevin Keegan in the Reds' side.

With Liverpool, Kenny became immensely popular, even more so than his predecessor. A richly talented forward, Dalglish is regarded as being amongst the very greatest players of the modern era. Totally determined and unselfish with the ball, he could be quite brilliant at finishing in front of goal and scored many spectacular efforts around the box. Dalglish grabbed

172 League and Cup goals for Liverpool – this on top of 167 for Celtic. Kenny totalled almost 900 senior games in his playing career. Additionally claiming more than 100 caps for his country – the most by any Scottish player – he also has scored most goals for Scotland too.

Dalglish helped Liverpool to a succession of titles, cup wins and moments of European glory before moving into the player-manager's role in June 1985, when he took over from Joe Fagan. And the Glasgow-born Scot proved equally successful as a boss. He achieved the double in his first season in charge, and led Liverpool for almost seven years before resigning in February 1991.

Deeply moved by two tragic events he witnessed at first hand – the European Cup final disaster at the Heysel Stadium in Belgium in 1985, and then the FA Cup semi-final tragedy at Hillsborough in 1989 – he left Anfield and went out of football for a period. But the lure of a post revitalizing Blackburn Rovers with the help of multi-millionaire Jack Walker tempted

It needed a hero to replace a hero and Kenny Dalglish certainly fitted the bill.

Dalglish back into management by the end of 1991.

With Rovers, Kenny established a set-up at Ewood Park that has taken the once-proud club back to the top of the game. He earned promotion into the Premier League, then signed quality players once in the elite – men such as Alan Shearer, David Batty and Tim Flowers. His reward came in 1995, when Rovers plucked the Premiership title from the grasp of Manchester United.

Surprisingly, however, Dalglish then shocked the football world again by moving out of the limelight when he was at the top. He soon moved to a back-room role at Ewood Park and left the club completely during 1996, later taking up a part-time position with Glasgow Rangers, the club he supported as a youth. Then the managership of Newcastle became available and with little hesitation Kenny accepted the post.

Though perhaps lacking Keegan's charm and flair, at least in the eyes of the outside world, Dalglish has many other first-class qualities. He commands the same level of respect that Keegan did, and in the opinion of

King Kenny on the training pitch, very much involved with the players.

Kenny DALGLISH

Born:
 Dalmarnock, Glasgow, 1951
Playing career:
 Glasgow Celtic, Liverpool.
Playing Honours:
 102 Scotland caps, 4 Scotland Under-23 caps.
 Scottish League champions 1972, 1973, 1974, 1977.
 Scottish Cup-winner 1972, 1974, 1975, 1977.
 Scottish Cup finalist 1973.
 Scottish League Cup-winner 1975.
 Scottish League Cup finalist 1972, 1973, 1974, 1977.
 Football League champions 1979, 1980, 1982, 1983, 1984.
 Football League Cup-winner 1981, 1982, 1983, 1984.
 Football League Cup finalist 1978.
 European Cup-winner 1978, 1981, 1984.
 European Cup finalist 1985.
 PFA Player of the Year 1983.
 FWA Footballer of the Year 1979, 1983.
 Awarded the MBE 1985.

Managerial Record:
 Liverpool, Blackburn Rovers, Newcastle United
Managerial Honours:
 Football League champions 1986, 1988, 1990, Premier League champions 1995, FA Cup-winner 1986, 1989, FA Cup finalist 1988, Football League Cup finalist 1987, Football League Div. 2 promotion 1992, Manager of the Year 1986, 1988, 1990.
Managerial Record:

1985–86	**Div 1**	Champs	FAC	Winners	LC	SF		
1986–87	**Div 1**	2nd	FAC	R3	LC	Finalists		
1987–88	**Div 1**	Champs	FAC	Finalists	LC	R3		
1988–89	**Div 1**	2nd	FAC	Winners	LC	R4		
1989–90	**Div 1**	Champs	FAC	SF	LC	R3		
1990–91	**Div 1**	2nd	FAC	–	LC	R3		
1991–92	**Div 2**	Promoted	FAC	R4	LC	–		
1992–93	**Prem Lg**	4th	FAC	R6	LC	SF		
1993–94	**Prem Lg**	2nd	FAC	R4	LC	R4		
1994–95	**Prem Lg**	Champs	FAC	R3	LC	R4	UEFAC	R1
1995–96	–	–	–	–	–	–		
1996–97	**Prem Lg**	2nd	FAC	R4	LC	–	UEFAC	QF

many is more tactically aware as a manager than his predecessor. Dalglish will send out a team to defend and snatch a win when he needs to; he'll attack all-out when he needs to; and he'll instil a level of discipline and work-rate which will ensure that when the Magpies are ahead, it will be difficult for any side to take away that advantage.

After gradually assessing the strengths and weaknesses of the whole playing set-up at St James' Park, Dalglish began to revitalise his staff following the club's second runners-up spot in succession. During the close season of 1997 players came and went as Kenny assembled a formidable squad to challenge again for Premiership, FA Cup and European trophies. And just as in Kevin Keegan's day, the squad is overflowing with international talent of the very best quality.

Chapter 7

Newcastle's Foreign Stars

Newcastle have never been afraid to bring in talent from overseas and United's Premiership squads have had glittering foreign stars.

There's only one Tino! Newcastle fans love the entertaining style of Colombian star Tino Asprilla.

Tino **Asprilla**

The £7.5 million purchase of Tino Asprilla from Italian club Parma during February 1996 was another record deal by United, and another transfer which stunned the Premiership as Newcastle reinforced their position as the big spenders of the game. The transfer was in fact surrounded in controversy, on, then off several times before eventually being sealed by all parties.

A highly-talented South American, Tino was quick to show his flamboyant skills to the Tyneside public, but it did take the Colombian several months to settle – and to understand English, never mind a Geordie accent! By the start of the 1996–97 season, however, Asprilla was well bedded in and beginning to add consistency to his performances especially in United's European fixtures, when he always raised his game to become a match-winner.

Newcastle were first attracted to Tino's unique style by his outstanding performances for Parma and the Colombian national squad. A one-off striker and nicknamed "the Black Arrow" in Italy, Asprilla can be explosive on the field with a sometimes-volatile

---

Tino ASPRILLA

Born: 10 November 1969, Tulua Valle, Colombia
Position: Striker
Height/weight: 5ft 7in/11st 3lb
Former clubs: Estudiantes de Tulua (Col), Deportivo Cali (Col), Atletico Nacional de Medellin (Col), Parma (Ita)
League & Cup appearances: 46
League & Cup goals: 12
International caps: 40-plus (Colombia)

David **Ginola**

Virtuoso David Ginola was a pin-up star with a great talent that almost took United to the title.

David GINOLA	
Born: 25 January 1967, Gassin, France	
Position: Outside-left/ midfield	
Height/weight: 6ft 11st/10lb	
Former clubs: Nice (Fra), Toulon (Fra), Matra Racing (Fra), Brest (Fra), Paris St-Germain (Fra)	
League & Cup appearances: 75	
League & Cup goals: 7	
International caps: 20 (France)	

The £2.5 million signing of David Ginola in July 1995 set Newcastle's fanatical Toon Army buzzing with expectation. Born near St Tropez, Ginola arrived on Tyneside as a player of experience with Paris St-Germain, having reached three European semi-finals, including the Champions' Cup in 1995. Appearing in almost 400 games in French football and winning several honours before crossing the Channel for the north-east, Ginola was clearly a virtuoso of the highest order, possessing lovely skills, poise and the ability to hit a telling cross or fire a stinging shot.

A former Footballer of the Year in France, the Frenchman was also something of a pin-up star – handsome, immaculately-dressed and a fashion model for the house of Cerutti as well! Tyneside's public loved him – both male and female – and his skills very nearly helped to bring the Championship trophy to Newcastle in the 1995–96 season. For the first half of that season, with the Magpies firing on all cylinders and leading the way in the title race, Ginola was quite devastating. On the left touchline, defenders could only hunt in packs to stop him delivering the ball for his team-mates, Ferdinand in particular, to cash in on.

Known as "Le Magnifique", and in the running for the Player of the Year Award that season, Ginola and the rest of his colleagues let the championship slip from their grasp by the end of the campaign. And Newcastle fans were never to see the best of the Frenchman again. Only in flashes was David on song: however, he did treat the Geordie crowd to special performances against Manchester United and Ferencvaros, 5–0 and 4–0 victories during 1996–97 which included two stunning goals from the Gallic genius.

Largely overlooked by his own national side while in England (a fate that also befell Eric Cantona), Ginola was very much a Keegan man, and by the time Kenny Dalglish was installed in the manager's chair at St James' Park David was destined to leave Tyneside.

temperament. To his credit, though, Tino has learned to control his Latin instincts in the Premier League and concentrated on making and scoring goals. His vision and speed in attack, as well as natural finishing in front of goal, have made him a most popular character with United's rank and file.

An entertainer, he specializes in an acrobatic somersault celebration on scoring a goal which delights spectators. Tino (full name Faustino) may appear leggy, loping and lazy on the field, but defenders know he can destroy them with a few seconds of mesmirizing skill. His unorthodox style of play confounds the opposition.

Footballer of the Year in his own country before moving from Colombia to Parma in the summer of 1992, Tino reached three European finals with the Italians and has also taken part in the 1990 and 1994 World Cups as well as the 1992 Olympic Games. A key figure in his country's bid to reach France in 1998, Asprilla is a player worthy of a world stage.

Philippe ALBERT

Born: 10 August 1967, Bouillon, Belgium
Position: Centre-half
Height/weight: 6ft 3in/13st
Former clubs: Dematter (Bel), Standard Bouillon (Bel), RSC Charleroi (Bel), KV Mechelen (Bel), RSC Anderlecht (Bel)
League & Cup appearances: 92
League & Cup goals: 12
International appearances: 40 (Belgium)

Everybody knows his name: Belgian star Philippe Albert is a cool, classy defender who often joins the attack with menace.

His style of play did not suit the new manager's requirements and after much transfer speculation he joined Tottenham Hotspur in July 1997 for a fee of more than £2 million. He was quickly reunited with his former Newcastle colleague, Les Ferdinand, when the centre-forward moved to White Hart Lane a matter of days later.

Philippe **Albert**

An established Belgian international, Philippe Albert had been a long-term target for Newcastle United, and during the 1994 World Cup in the USA Kevin Keegan saw Albert at first hand, standing out as a player of special quality. Within weeks of the Magpies' boss returning from the States the tall and commanding Belgian had become a Newcastle player for a fee of £2.65 million.

Cool and confident on the ball, he is a defender who can attack too, in the Continental fashion, striding forward from the middle of the defence with style. But he is also a tough, no-nonsense stopper and can handle the hottest of centre-forwards. Albert has an exquisite left foot, and much of Newcastle's passing game starts from his control and vision at the back.

A European thoroughbred (he appeared for his country in the 1990 World Cup as well) Philippe immediately became another Toon Army favourite at St James' Park with his classy ability. Having recovered from a serious cruciate ligament injury, the Belgian is always capable of scoring when he joins the attack. A free-kick expert, Albert has netted some wonderful goals for United: one special moment, which will live for years, came against Manchester United when he coolly chipped Peter Schmeichel from 25 yards.

Brought up in the Ardennes, Philippe won championship and cup honours with his country's top side, Anderlecht, and was voted Player of the Year in 1992.

Pavel **Srnicek**

A former Eastern Bloc soldier, Pavel Srnicek's arrival in the North-East during December 1990 for trials coincided with some of the poorest Newcastle displays on record, as the Magpies struggled in the old Division Two. At the time the tall, well-built keeper could speak little English and Pavel had a torrid early spell in United's side. However, Srnicek was determined to succeed.

The Czech gradually settled on Tyneside, learned English and improved his all-round goalkeeping skills, especially on the cross-ball. His progress was such that when Kevin Keegan took over the chair at Newcastle, Pavel claimed the Number One position, even though Mike Hooper was soon purchased as first choice.

Acrobatic and with exceptional shot-stopping ability, Pav earned something of a cult following with United's crowd with a series of spectacular saves as Newcastle entered the Premiership in 1993. One against Everton, in which he twisted in mid-air, even prompted the legendary Gordon Banks to vote it one of his Top Ten greatest saves!

Srnicek, who was Ludo Miklosko's deputy in the Banik team, reached his country's international side and was part of the Czech squad during the Euro '96 championships. But Pav always had a constant battle to keep the first-team shirt at St James' Park. He saw off Hooper, only for Shaka Hislop and, more recently, Shay Given to come into the side. That competition has been frustrating for Srnicek and he reluctantly almost quit Tyneside during the close-season of 1997.

Pavel SRNICEK

Born: 10 March 1968, Bohumin, Czechoslovakia
Position: Goalkeeper
Height/weight: 6ft 2in/14st 7lb
Former clubs: ZD Bohumin (Cze), Dukla Tabur (Cze), Dukla Prague (Cze), Banik Ostrava (Cze)
League & Cup appearances: 180
League & Cup goals: 0
International caps: 9 (Czech Republic)

Almost a cult hero on Tyneside, United fans have given Pavel Srnicek his own Geordie passport!

Marc **Hottiger**

The first of Kevin Keegan's two signings from the 1994 USA World Cup, along with Philippe Albert, Marc Hottiger had stood out for Switzerland in that tournament and carried the bargain price of £520,000. With more than 60 caps to his name, Hottiger was an established international full-back, and to pick up a player with such experience for that small amount of money was good business.

From the French-speaking part of Switzerland, Hottiger was a regular in United's Premiership line-up in 1994–95, showing a cool attitude in the right-back role and demonstrating the attacking urge, like most of Keegan's purchases. Although Marc had not performed badly, the manager felt his position was one which could be strengthened and the Magpies spent £4 million on a rival in the shape of Warren Barton the following summer. Together with the emergence of Steve Watson as a full-back of note, Hottiger found he had two stern rivals for a first-team place.

By the time Marc played for Switzerland during the Euro '96 festival in the UK, he had been transferred to Everton, picked up by Joe Royle for a fee of £700,000 in March 1996. The transfer though nearly didn't go through because of problems over work permits for a non-European Community national. Matters were resolved, but the Swiss full-back couldn't hold down a first-team place at Goodison Park either, appearing on only a handful of occasions for the Merseyside club.

Marc HOTTIGER

Born: 7 November 1967, Lausanne, Switzerland
Position: Right-back
Height/weight: 5ft 10in/11st 0lb
Former clubs: Renens (Swi), Lausanne Sports (Swi), FC Sion (Swi)
League & Cup appearances: 54
League & Cup goals: 2
International caps: 64 (Switzerland)

Left: Swiss international Marc Hottiger was purchased as result of his excellent performances in the 1994 World Cup. Opposite: Temur Ketsbaia is another experienced foreign import who has played the game around the world.

Temur **Ketsbaia**

Newcastle United manager Kenny Dalglish used the new transfer ruling very much to the club's benefit when he landed the established Georgian international Temur Ketsbaia. The £4 million-rated midfielder moved from top Greek club AEK Athens to Tyneside in July 1997 on a free transfer after his contract had expired, and the Magpies reaped the reward of the controversial Bosman ruling.

With more than 20 caps for his country, the balding Ketsbaia decided to join the Black-and-Whites after considering offers from top sides in Germany, Spain and Italy. With a football brain and non-stop engine, Temur had little hesitation in selecting St James' Park, seeing the Premiership and Newcastle United as the place to be.

The Georgian national started his footballing career as a striker and made his mark in the old Soviet football network with the respected Dinamo Tbilisi club. After winning honours in the USSR he moved abroad to Cyprus and Greece, teaming up with AEK Athens in 1994. He helped lift the Greek domestic cup in 1996 and 1997 and has been a regular in European action for several years, displaying his brand of football for both club and country all over the world.

Fast on and off the ball, his penetrating runs from midfield give United's side a boost. Without doubt he will soon become a new star of the Premiership and may become as well known as his compatriot, friend and international team-mate playing at Manchester City, Georgiou Kinkladze.

Temur KETSBAIA

Born: 18 March 1968, Gale, Georgia
Position: Midfield
Former clubs: Dinamo Sukhumi (Geo), Dinamo Tbilisi (Geo), Anorthosis Famagusta (Cyp), AEK Athens (Gre)
League & Cup appearances: 0
League & Cup goals: 0
International caps: 22 (Georgia)

Danish Golden Boy – Jon Tomasson could become one of the biggest Premiership names of the future.

Jon **Tomasson**

Many noted judges of football in Denmark and Holland rated the talent of Jon Dahl Tomasson very highly as Newcastle United took a close interest in the young forward. The 21-year-old had just broken into the Danish national side and after almost three years in Dutch football with Heerenveen had proved to be an exciting new talent on the scene – good enough to be the new star of Danish football.

Jon TOMASSON	
Born:	29 August 1976, Copenhagen, Denmark
Position:	Striker/midfield
Former clubs:	Solrod (Den), Koge (Den), Heerenveen (Hol)
League & Cup appearances:	0
League & Cup goals:	0
International caps:	3 (Denmark)

Kenny Dalglish and Terry McDermott were determined to bring him to St James' Park. Tall, skilful and with coolness of a seasoned pro on the ball, Tomasson likes to operate just behind the front striker and combines effectively in both attack and in midfield. Newcastle moved quickly as the 1996–97 season closed and succeeded in signing the player in the face of stiff competition from the likes of Real Madrid, Ajax, Barcelona and Monaco. He was hot property, and the £2.2 million fee was quickly shown to be money very well spent as Tomasson started to show the quality he had displayed in Holland, and for Denmark, to United's fans as well as to a wider audience in the Premiership.

A clinical finisher, Jon began his career as a 15-year-old with Solrod, his home-town club just outside of Copenhagen. He will be a player to watch in the coming seasons; a huge star in the making.

Alessandro **Pistone**

One of the brightest prospects in Italy's Serie A, Alessandro Pistone arrived on Tyneside during July 1997 for a £4.3 million fee. A talented defender, able to operate in the centre of the defence, at left-back, or in a wing-back role, Pistone had been a target of the Magpies for a long time. A change in management at the San Siro alerted United that he might be available, and the player was delighted to move to England.

A former captain of the Italian Under-21 side, he is tipped for a full call-up for his country and is used to performing at the highest level, both in Italian football and in European competition. With Inter Milan since 1995, 22-year-old Alessandro helped the Italians reach the UEFA Cup Final in 1997 before moving to England. Tall, cultured on the ball and with great composure, Pistone is quick going forward and in recovery and has been taken to heart by the Geordie crowd – including the North-East's many Italian citizens. He had a spell with Vicenza and Crevalcora as a youngster and will strengthen United's defence immensely this season.

Alessandro PISTONE	
Born:	27 July 1975, Milan, Italy
Position:	Defender
Former clubs:	Crevalcora, (Ita) Vicenza (Ita), Inter Milan (Ita)
League & Cup appearances:	0
League & Cup goals:	0
International caps:	Italy Under-21

Alessandro Pistone is a formidable defender who is quick, positive and an excellent passer too.

Chapter 8

The Stars of the Future

When he was a boy Alan Shearer went to St James' Park to watch his United heroes. Today's youth will be tomorrow's stars.

The North-East of England has long been regarded as a hotbed of soccer talent, and over the years has produced hundreds of top footballers. In modern times, the players such as Manchester United's Bryan Robson and Steve Bruce have graced the field and Newcastle have fielded a string of superstars; Chris Waddle, Paul Gascoigne, Peter Beardsley and of course Alan Shearer, all Geordies through and through. They are part of a long tradition: Bobby and Jack Charlton, Bobby Robson and Jackie Milburn are only four of many, many tremendous players hailing from the North-East who have won glory on British and foreign fields.

However, Newcastle's youth policy over the years has been rightly criticized. Too many North-East lads drifted from their own backyard to clubs elsewhere, having failed to get a chance with United. Now the club recognizes that in order to compete with the best in Europe, a structured youth scheme needs to be in place and given the highest priority, capturing local talent and mixing home-grown products with star signings.

For a while, Kevin Keegan disbanded United's Central League side and concentrated on big buys. Kenny Dalglish reintroduced a reserve structure and

has now expanded the youth set-up. Within a short while the Magpies will have several youth teams operating in the region, and in many age groups. The club's Centre of Excellence, managed by John Carver and John Murray, and its Football in the Community scheme, run by former Leeds striker Ray Hankin – a Geordie himself – are important parts of that policy.

Former Celtic boss Tommy Burns arrived at St James' Park in the summer of 1997.

Centre of Excellence

On the St James' Park staff at present are several youngsters well worth watching in the coming months. A mixture of teenagers purchased by Kenny Dalglish as players of special quality and lads taken on at St James' Park from school, they are looked after by a coaching staff full of top-level experience. Ex-Newcastle United player Terry McDermott has won virtually every honour in the game, many alongside Kenny Dalglish in a long period with his home-town side of Liverpool. Now assistant manager to Dalglish, he gives the kids lots of advice as one would expect from a man who collected both the PFA and FWA Footballer of the Year awards in 1980.

In coach Tommy Burns, who joined United during the summer of 1997 after leaving Celtic, Newcastle has another former player and manager boasting a record few can match. Burns appeared in midfield for Celtic on more than 500 occasions and won championship and cup medals galore in Scotland. He was at Parkhead as a youngster when Kenny Dalglish wore the famous green and white hoops of Celtic.

Alan Irvine is another Scot now walking the corridors of St James' Park. Born in Glasgow, like Dalglish and Burns, Alan played for Queen's Park, Everton, Crystal Palace, Dundee United and Blackburn Rovers in a career that saw the forward appear at Wembley in the Merseyside derby League Cup Final in 1984.

Irvine entered coaching with Dalglish at Blackburn and has moved to St James' Park to look after United's youth policy.

Chris McMenemy – son of former Southampton boss Lawrie – is also on the coaching staff, as are John Murray and John Carver. Murray and Carver are both Tyneside men, and both are steeped in football. Murray appeared for Burnley and Blackpool, as well as Bury, Reading and Brentford, while Carver started his career with the Magpies back in 1982 alongside Kevin Keegan, before moving to Cardiff City.

Newcastle United's youth schemes are now strong and a network of local, national and international scouts is permanently on the lookout for footballing talent. Although the Magpies have lifted the prestigious FA Youth Cup only twice, in 1962 and 1985, that may all change in the future. It is clear that success in that competition breeds success, as Manchester United have proved over the years; and the two sides which brought the cup home to St James' Park for United were full of players who went on to make the grade.

In 1961–62 Newcastle's youth line-up contained David Craig and Bobby Moncur, who both became regular international players with United. There too was Alan Suddick, a golden boy for many a year on Tyneside who developed into a highly talented player. Colin Clish, John Markie and Dave Turner went on to have fine careers elsewhere, as did Les O'Neil.

The 1984–85 winning team was led by a confident and highly skilled Paul Gascoigne who of course became one of the country's biggest-ever footballing personalities. Other players to go on to even greater things were Joe Allon, Brian Tinnion, Tony Nesbit, Jeff Wrightson, Paul Stephenson and Kevin Scott, who tallied more than 200 games for the Magpies.

Bjarni **Gudjonsson**

Newcastle tracked the teenage star of Icelandic football for several months before securing a deal that brought the 18-year-old to Tyneside for a fee of £250,000. Gudjonsson had been to St James' Park twice for trials during the 1996–97 season and on both occasions impressed the Magpies' management. He was also wanted by several other clubs, including Liverpool and Real Madrid, netting a hat-trick for the Spanish giants in a friendly. Bjarni has a good turn of speed up-front, and although only five feet eight inch-

Youth Team Successes

Youth Cup Final 1962	Youth Cup Final 1985
Wolves 1 Newcastle United 1	Newcastle United 0 Watford 0
United goalscorer: Chapman	**Att:** 5,774
Att: 13,916	
	Watford 1 Newcastle United 4
Newcastle United 1 Wolves 0	**United goalscorers:** Allon 2,
United goalscorer: Moncur	Gascoigne 2
Att: 20,588	**Att:** 7,087
Newcastle won on aggregate 2–1	Newcastle won 4–1 on aggregate
United: Craig S, Craig D, Clish, Chapman, Markie, Turner, Gowlands, Suddick, Watkin, Moncur, O'Neil.	**United:** Kelly, Dickenson, Tinnion, Nesbit, Scott, Kilford, Hayton, Gascoigne, Allon, Forster, Wrightson. Sub: Stephenson.

es tall can cause defenders problems with his skill and awareness. An Under-21 international for Iceland, he helped his previous club Akranes to their domestic League championship in 1997. Born into a footballing family, Gudjonsson's father coached Akranes while his brother played soccer in Germany and now in Belgium.

Baby-faced Icelander Bjarni Gudjonsson looks even younger than his 18 years.

Brian **Pinas**

A Dutch youth international with lots of ability, winger Brian Pinas was captured in July 1997. Joining the Magpies from top Netherlands club Feyenoord, Pinas's acquisition shows that Newcastle's youth network operates effectively far from the Tyne. With the talent to become quite a star in the skilful Dutch mould, Pinas is one player many supporters will be carefully tracking in the coming months.

Patrick **Kelly**

Newcastle picked up the former Celtic youngster during the summer of 1997 after his contract at Parkhead expired. First spotted by Dalglish when Kelly was playing alongside his own son in the Celtic youth side, the highly-rated youngster has made his debut in Scottish football, appearing for the Celts' first eleven last season. Hailing from Kirkcaldy in Fife, Kelly is a midfielder of considerable promise.

Paul **Brayson**

Paul Brayson has scored more than 100 goals for United's youth and reserve line-ups since joining the Magpies from schools football in July 1994. Nicknamed "Brassy", the slightly-built Geordie forward has a natural touch on the ball and underwent his first-team baptism in a League Cup tie against Bristol City during the 1995–96 season. A regular at the FA's training complex at Lilleshall, Brayson has reached the England youth side. A local youngster

Paul Brayson, born and bred near St James' Park, could become the next local lad to succeed.

brought up in the shadow of St James' Park, Paul could well impress Kenny Dalglish in the coming months after gaining experience on loan with Swansea for a spell during 1996–97.

Aaron **Hughes**

Born in Northern Ireland and raised in Cookstown, Aaron Hughes is probably the brightest prospect in United's junior squad. Destined to be called up for the full international side in the 1997–98 season, the tall defender has shown all the qualities needed to become a Premiership player. At the age of 15 he was on schoolboy forms with the Magpies after being snatched from the grasp of Manchester United, where he spent some time. An Irish youth international, Hughes possesses the right attitude to succeed and it will be no surprise if Aaron makes his Premier League debut in the coming season.

David **Burt**

Born in Blyth, David Burt is a very pacey and skilful forward: indeed, some have called him another Keith Gillespie. First discovered playing for Bedlington Juniors in Northumberland, United missed him and he went to The Hawthorns and tried his luck with West Bromwich Albion. But the teenager did not settle in the Midlands, longing to be back in the North-East, and Newcastle, where his brother Jamie was also on the books, stepped in and signed David on YTS terms. Able to get past defenders, Burt can deliver a good cross from the right flank and has been included in Newcastle's first-team squad during the 1996–97 season.

Paul **Barratt**

A midfielder, Paul Barratt was born a long goal-kick from St James' Park and has, as they say, black-and-white blood. Previously with the Walker Central youth side, Barratt has since developed into a tall playmaker with good vision who excels, at passing, both long and short. Good enough to get into the England Under-18 side, Paul has travelled with the first team and, now that the club has a Central League eleven once more, will benefit from the experience gained against seasoned professionals.

Aaron Hughes will be a cool and polished presence in the heart of Newcastle's defence in the future.

Chapter 9

The Great Matches

In four seasons of Premiership action, there have been enough great matches to fill a whole book, such has been the impact of "The Entertainers", Newcastle United.

NEWCASTLE UNITED 4 (2)
CHELSEA 2 (2)

FA Premier League

Saturday 10 September 1994, St James' Park

This pulsating match was played at St James' Park on a glorious, sunny afternoon and it featured four goals inside the opening half-hour of the contest. The match got off to a terrific start when Andy Cole was sent through on the corner of the box. The Magpies' centre-forward rocketed a left-foot shot past Kharine and into the top of the net. It was one of the goals of the season.

But Chelsea were a stylish side, too, and they hit back almost immediately. Former Newcastle favourite Gavin Peacock collected a loose ball in the box to net after Hooper had made a great save from Dennis Wise, who was later sent off. It was up to the other end of the field as the two teams attacked and counter-attacked in an end-to-end affair. After 20 minutes Andy Cole was felled by Steve Clarke in the penalty area and Rob Lee fired a spot-kick which was parried – but Ruel Fox ran in to score from the rebound.

The match swayed again as Chelsea claimed a second equalizer before the interval. A deep cross caught Newcastle's defence out and Paul Furlong rose to loop a header over Mike Hooper. Newcastle's team-talk in the dressing-room was effective. After losing the lead twice they were in no mood to let Chelsea off the hook for a third time.

Slick interplay in midfield gave Lee an opening and he buried the chance. The England midfielder was back in the 66th minute, giving the ball to Cole who decisively concluded the match with Newcastle's fourth goal. Chelsea' keeper Dmitri Kharine could do nothing to stop the clinical finishing by the former Arsenal junior. Newcastle won the contest 4–2. The match was compulsive viewing, with two well-matched clubs playing open, attacking football.

Kevin Keegan commented: "At 2–2 it could have gone either way. But it was fantastic entertainment". Entertainment it certainly was from two clubs that have been at the forefront of providing the public with value for money in the Premier League.

NEWCASTLE UNITED 4 (2) CHELSEA 2 (2)

United: Hooper, Hottiger, Beresford, Venison, Peacock, Albert, Fox, Watson, Lee, Cole, Sellars.
Subs not used: Burridge, Howey, Mathie.

Goals: Cole (7, 66), Fox (20), Lee (53).

Chelsea: Kharine, Clarke, Sinclair, Kjeldjerg, Johnsen, Wise, Spackman (Newton), Spencer, Rocastle (Hoddle), Peacock, Furlong.
Sub not used: Colgan.

Goals: Peacock (15), Furlong (28).

Att: 34,435

Andy Cole takes the ball around Chelsea goalkeeper Dmitri Kharine during the Magpies' 4–2 victory over the Blues at St James' Park. Cole opened and closed the scoring.

Darren Peacock (between Spurs players, right) scores Newcastle's second goal of the opening 10 minutes at St James' Park. However, United were 3–2 behind after just 26 minutes.

NEWCASTLE UNITED 3 (2)
TOTTENHAM HOTSPUR 3 (3)

FA Premier League

Wednesday 3 May 1995, St James' Park

Newcastle's opening burst in this match would have destroyed most sides as United attacked the Spurs defence in brilliant style. Storming forward at every opportunity, they were 2–0 ahead within 10 minutes! A great run and cross from Steve Watson on the left touchline saw Keith Gillespie head the ball past Ian Walker. Then three minutes later Spurs were under fire again, as more pressure resulted in a corner and Beardsley's kick saw Darren Peacock head in for a rare goal by Newcastle's centre-half.

United could have claimed more goals, but were rocked themselves as Spurs started to link up front. Nick Barmby worked a one-two with Jürgen

Klinsman and slipped the ball into United's net to start a remarkable come-back in double-quick time. Two minutes later a cross was swung over the Magpies' defence for Klinsmann to pick the ball up at the far post and drill a low shot past Srnicek.

The game was very much in Spurs' court now and

NEWCASTLE UTD 3 (2) TOTTENHAM HOTSPUR 3 (3)

United: Srnicek, Hottiger, Beresford, Bracewell (Allen), Peacock, Howey, Fox (Hooper), Lee, Watson, Beardsley, Gillespie.
Sub not used: Clark.

Tottenham Hotspur: Walker, Austin, Edinburgh, Howells, Mabbutt, Calderwood, Barmby (Campbell), Anderton, Sheringham, Klinsmann, Rosenthal.
Subs not used: Thorstvedt, Nethercott.

Goals: Gillespie (7), Peacock (10), Beardsley (70).

Att: 35,603

Goals: Barmby (22), Klinsmann (24), Anderton (26).

immediately after their equalizer, Darren Anderton unleashed a 30-yard screamer into the top of the net. After being 2–0 behind, the Londoners were now 3–2 ahead! The Magpies couldn't believe it and went into the dressing-room for the break astonished.

The second half of this fantastic 90 minutes of football was no less dramatic. Newcastle found their form again in a game that swayed back and forth. Chances came and went before Nick Barmby was clipped by Pavel Srnicek in the box as he tried to go round the big United 'keeper. The Czech was controversially sent off, and straight away Mike Hooper came off the bench. The first thing he had to do was face a Klinsmann penalty. Amazingly, United's substitute keeper made a great save to keep Newcastle in the game. He then further delighted spectators by stopping a shot from Anderton before Spurs themselves had a man – defender Colin Calderwood – ordered off.

Now Newcastle had the scent of not only an equalizer but a victory and, backed by a crowd yelling themselves hoarse in support, United grabbed a goal from Peter Beardsley who sneaked in ahead of Sol Campbell to level at 3–3. The winner didn't come, though, and a draw was a fair result for this epic clash.

Peter Beardsley commented later, "In the end the spoils were shared and we all got a cheer. It was some night...with the atmosphere the best I've ever experienced in my two spells at St James' Park".

LIVERPOOL 4 (1)
NEWCASTLE UNITED 3 (2)
FA Premier League
Wednesday 3 April 1996, Anfield

Apart from pitting two of the Premiership's finest teams against one another, this match was also crucial to the title race. Newcastle and Liverpool were challenging Manchester United's title and points were valuable. A lot was at stake and both sides played with attacking flair in a match that has gone down in history as the best since the whole Premier League started.

Newcastle were a goal down inside the second minute when Stan Collymore did well to cross a dangerous ball and Fowler headed in at the far post.

LIVERPOOL 4 (1) NEWCASTLE UNITED 3 (2)

Liverpool: James, Jones (Rush), Wright (Harkness), Ruddock, Scales, McAteer, Redknapp, McManaman, Fowler, Collymore, Barnes.
Sub not used: Warner.

Goals: Fowler (2, 54), Collymore (67, 90).

United: Srnicek, Watson, Beresford, Howey (Peacock), Albert, Batty, Lee, Beardsley, Ferdinand, Asprilla, Ginola.
Subs not used: Clark, Gillespie.

Goals: Ferdinand (9), Ginola (13), Asprilla (56).

Att: 40,702

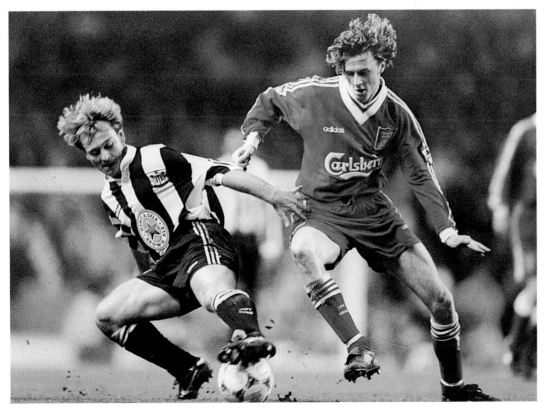

Matches between Newcastle and Liverpool have been marvellous contests since United joined the Premier League. In April 1996, the game was an epic. United's John Beresford tackles the Reds' Steve McManaman during the 90 minutes of scintillating football of the highest order which culminated in Stan Collymore's winner in the dying moments of the match. A year later, the teams repeated the dose in another classic.

Newcastle, though, were inspired, and came at Liverpool in their own camp. After nine minutes Tino Asprilla took on Neil Ruddock, went past him and pulled the ball back for Les Ferdinand to whack the ball over James and into the net.

With that goal the Magpies had their tails up, and four minutes later went 2–1 ahead with a glorious goal. Ferdinand collected the ball in the centre of the field to send David Ginola through with only James to beat. The Frenchman kept his head and the ball settled in the back of the net. The Newcastle fans watching – and millions on television – thought United had done enough to claim a share of the game for their title challenge. But the pulsating match was far from over.

On the restart, it was Liverpool's turn to show their quality and they hit an equalizer when Steve McManaman squared the ball to Fowler, who struck an 18-yard shot into the left corner of Srnicek's goal. But Newcastle wouldn't submit, and immediately took the lead once more when a Rob Lee pass split the home defence for Asprilla, who brilliantly curled his shot round the onrushing James.

Yet Liverpool hit back this time, and on 67 minutes McAteer's low cross was forced in at the far post by Collymore to make the contest 3–3. Everyone reckoned that was it, but remarkably in the very last minute Barnes found Collymore and the Liverpool striker blasted the winner past Pavel Srnicek from ten yards.

Kevin Keegan commented; "A classic in terms of entertainment, but it was cruel to lose a game after you have played so well".

NEWCASTLE UNITED 5 (2)
MANCHESTER UNITED 0 (0)
FA Premier League
Sunday 20 October 1996, St James' Park

Following Manchester United's title victory in a chase with the Magpies during the 1995–96 season, and their 4–0 drubbing of the Black-and-Whites at Wembley in the Charity Shield, Newcastle needed a good display against their Premiership rivals. And the Toon Army

The Red Devils are under the cosh – and it's about to get worse as Alan Shearer fires in United's fourth.

Les Ferdinand rises to meet Alan Shearer's cross and powers a header into the Manchester United net.

certainly enjoyed this 5–0 destruction of the Reds.

The Magpies were on their game during the opening exchanges and the crucial midfield battle was being won by Batty and Lee. Newcastle got the important opening goal in the 12th minute thanks to the eagle eyes of the referee and his assistant. In a goalmouth scramble, Darren Peacock headed the ball towards the Manchester goal-line but it appeared to have been cleared. However, the officials awarded the goal, as the whole ball had just sneaked over the line.

Flying high – Les Ferdinand is unchallenged as he scores Newcastle's second goal against Aston Villa with a great header from Keith Gillespie's tantalizing cross. Villa's late fightback came up just a little short.

NEWCASTLE UTD 5 (2) MANCHESTER UTD 0 (0)

United: Srnicek, Watson (Barton), Peacock, Albert, Beresford, Batty, Lee (Clark), Beardsley, Ginola, Shearer, Ferdinand.
Subs not used: Asprilla, Gillespie, Hislop.

Goals: Peacock (12), Ginola (30), Ferdinand (62), Shearer (74), Albert (83).

Manchester United: Schmeichel, Neville G, May, Pallister, Irwin, Johnsen (Scholes), Beckham, Poborsky (McClair), Butt, Solskjaer (Cruyff), Cantona.
Subs not used: Neville P, Van der Gouw.

Att: 36,579

The Sky television replays indicated that the decision had been the correct one.

There was little doubt about Newcastle's second goal, though, when David Ginola received the ball with his back to goal on the edge of the visitor's box. A turn and shot, and the ball flew into Schmeichel's net. Then Shearer thudded another shot against the base of the post. Newcastle walked off for the interval to a standing ovation.

The second half was more of the same. United totally controlled the match and rarely let the Old Trafford club in with a chance. In attack, too, the Magpies were awesome. Alan Shearer destroyed the Reds' defence in a wing run and his marvellous cross was met by Les Ferdinand, who powered a header into the net. Then Shearer arrived on the scoresheet himself after both Beardsley and Ferdinand had shots saved by Schmeichel.

Newcastle's scintillating display was capped with a glorious fifth goal from Philippe Albert in the 83rd minute. Following nice possession interplay by the Magpies, Albert collected the ball deep. The Belgian international took a few strides forward, noticed Schmeichel off his line and coolly chipped a brilliant 25-yard shot over the Danish 'keeper into the net.

Kevin Keegan commented: "We showed what we are about today. We're certainly a team worth paying money to watch".

Newcastle's display earned them the tag of title favourites from the bookies. Up front, the partnership of England teammates, Shearer and Ferdinand was proving devastating, while the support play of Ginola, Beardsley, Lee and Batty gave Newcastle both a creative and solid look. However, championships are not won or lost on single performances, no matter how good or bad. In the end, Manchester United had the last laugh, and the Magpies had to settle for a second consecutive runners-up spot.

NEWCASTLE UNITED 4 (3) ASTON VILLA 3 (1)

FA Premier League
Monday 30 September 1996, St James' Park

Sky Television have certainly had their money's-worth from featuring Newcastle United in the Premiership, and this broadcast was among the best. The match with Aston Villa twisted and turned throughout the 90 minutes and began with a bang – two goals inside the first five minutes!

Dwight Yorke, who put on a formidable display all evening, silenced the noisy St James' Park crowd after just four minutes. He headed a cross past Srnicek, but it took Newcastle all of 73 seconds to equalize when Les Ferdinand sent the ball past keeper Michael Oakes at the far post following Shearer's opening. From then on, Newcastle had the upper hand for the rest of the half. Keith Gillespie crossed well and Ferdinand converted the chance with a great header.

United's superiority was reinforced when Alan Shearer snapped up a loose chance after Ferdinand's shot had been blocked on the line. Newcastle were 3–1 ahead and, with Mark Draper sent off, were cruising to three points.

Dramatically, however, 10-man Villa shook the Magpies after the break. Yorke scored a tremendous solo goal on the hour to pull the deficit back to 3–2. The game then swung back to the Tynesiders when Steve Howey headed his first goal of the season from a Gillespie cross. Yet it was Villa who finished the stronger.

Yorke, however, wasn't finished. Within two minutes of Howey's goal the Villa striker was back at the other end firing the ball past Srnicek to put the game back in the melting pot at 4–3 and collect his hat-trick. The fixture very nearly ended in an amazing 4–4 draw, when another Yorke effort found the net but was chalked off for offside.

NEWCASTLE UNITED 4 (3) ASTON VILLA 3 (1)

United: Srnicek, Watson, Peacock, Howey, Beresford, Batty, Lee, Ginola(Asprilla), Gillespie, Ferdinand, Shearer.
Subs not used: Albert, Elliott, Kitson, Hislop.

Goals: Ferdinand (5, 22), Shearer (38), Howey (67).

Aston Villa: Oakes, Nelson, Ehiogu, Southgate, Staunton, Wright, Taylor, Draper, Curcic, Milosevic, Yorke.
Subs not used: Johnson, Joachim, Hendrie, Scimeca, Rachel.

Goals: Yorke (4, 59, 69).
Att: 36,400

NEWCASTLE UNITED 7 (2)
TOTTENHAM HOTSPUR 1 (0)
FA Premier League
Saturday 28 December 1996, St James' Park

Newcastle, and Kevin Keegan in particular, needed a festive-season boost at a difficult time in the club's Premiership history, and poor Spurs felt the full force of the Magpie goal machine. United had gone seven games without a win and their title challenge had faded, but this seven-goal romp changed all that.

Tottenham's defence crumbled as soon as Alan Shearer held off challenges from Carr and Calderwood to hit a right-foot volley over Tottenham goalkeeper Walker. Three minutes later the floodgates started to open, after Peter Beardsley's shot was diverted by Les Ferdinand into Spurs' net. Then 13 minutes into the second half John Beresford went on a run down the left touchline and crossed for Ferdinand to sweep the ball past Walker again.

United's fourth arrived rapidly and it was a fine goal from Rob Lee. United's midfield general ended a run from deep by driving the ball low and hard past the helpless Spurs keeper from 15 yards. The next goal came 18 minutes later and proved a historic moment – the club's 6,000th League strike! Philippe Albert was the man to grab it, joining in the attack and finding himself unmarked when Lee returned the ball to him. The Belgian drilled it under the advancing Walker.

In the closing minutes Newcastle went on the rampage and could have scored more than the two they

---

NEWCASTLE UTD 7 (2)   TOTTENHAM HOTSPUR 1 (0)

United: Hislop, Watson, Peacock, Albert, Beresford, Batty, Lee, Gillespie (Clark), Beardsley, Shearer, Ferdinand.
Subs not used: Srnicek, Kitson, Elliott, Crawford.

Goals: Shearer (19, 82), Ferdinand (22, 58), Lee (60, 87), Albert (78).

Tottenham Hotspur: Walker, Carr, Calderwood, Campbell, Wilson, Fox, Howells, Nielson, Sinton (Dozzell [Rosenthal]), Iversen, Sheringham.
Subs not used: Baardsen, Nethercott, Austin.

Goal: Neilsen (88).

Att: 36,308

Shear power – Alan Shearer holds off challenges from two Tottenham defenders to volley United into a 19th-minute lead at St James' Park. It opened the floodgates for a goal deluge.

got as Tottenham's defence disintegrated. Alan Shearer scored the sixth by volleying home David Batty's pass from close range, then Lee received another Batty pass to pick his spot from the edge of the box. Spurs did manage a single consolation effort in the dying moments, Allan Neilsen stabbing into the net after Hislop had saved from Teddy Sheringham.

A 7–1 result was very satisfying for United, and Tottenham deserve credit for playing an open game. Their defence, though, was ravaged.

Terry McDermott made the comment; "Apart from the goals, we had a lot of other chances and the score could have been doubled".

It was the perfect end to a pretty good year.

NEWCASTLE UNITED 4 (1)
LEICESTER CITY 3 (0)
FA Premier League
Sunday 2 February 1997, St James' Park

Recent fixtures against Leicester City have usually been quite dramatic affairs, both at St James' Park and at Filbert Street. The clash on Tyneside during February 1997 was typical. United were 1–0 ahead, then 3–1 behind, only to win a stirring game through an Alan Shearer hat-trick in the last 14 minutes of play!

The two Elliotts on the field, Robbie for United and Matt for City, gave the match the opening goals in what was, for the first hour, a close-run thing. But then the fireworks really started to happen. After grabbing the equalizer in the 55th minute, Leicester went at Newcastle in earnest and scored rapid goals through Claridge and Heskey. City's 14-minute burst rocked St James' Park.

With Newcastle now 3–1 down, manager Kenny Dalglish sent on David Ginola from the bench and the Frenchman gave United a much-needed boost. He danced round one tackle but then was fouled on the edge of the box. Alan Shearer stepped up to belt in the free kick with a humdinger of a shot that flew past Leicester's American goalkeeper Kasey Keller.

With the backing of a crowd sensing something special, United charged at City with all guns blazing.

Shearer received the ball just inside the box. He turned and struck another shot which found its way inside the post to level the game at 3–3.

Now it was Leicester who were shell-shocked. Newcastle powered forward, and as the game entered injury time some lovely interplay sent Lee through to pull the ball back for that man Shearer, who stroked the ball over the line for the winner. And it could have been five, when Keller went into attack and was left stranded 80 yards from goal! Ginola's 55-yard chip at the empty net drifted just wide.

Newcastle's tremendous comeback from the dead was complete. Leicester City manager Martin O'Neill could not believe it. Neither could Kenny Dalglish.

United's manager commented: "Alan got the three goals, but everyone showed a great resolve. Every single one of them deserves praise".

NEWCASTLE UNITED 4 (1)	LEICESTER CITY 3 (0)
United: Hislop, Watson, Peacock, Albert, Elliott R, Batty, Lee, Gillespie (Ginola), Asprilla (Clark), Shearer, Ferdinand.	**Leicester City:** Keller, Grayson, Watts, Prior, Elliott M, Taylor (Lawrence), Izzett, Lennon, Parker, Claridge, Heskey.
Subs not used: Srnicek, Beardsley, Barton.	**Subs not used:** Poole, Robins, Hill, Wilson.
Goals: Elliott R (3), Shearer (76, 83, 90).	**Goals:** Elliott M (55), Claridge (60), Heskey (68).
Att: 36,396	

Left: It may have been from close range, but Alan Shearer sends the ball over the goalline and Newcastle fans into raptures. It is the winning goal in the 4–3 defeat of Leicester City and it completed Shearer's 14-minute hat-trick.
Right: Goalkeeper Kasey Keller looks aghast as Shearer's 83rd-minute shot creeps inside the post to go in for United's equalizer. Leicester had led 3–1 with 22 minutes to go.

Chapter 10

At Home

Newcastle United's home, St James' Park, is the oldest football stadium in the region. Situated on a hill overlooking the city, close to the former site of public hangings – hence the name Gallowgate. It first staged an organized game of football in 1880.

The ground was then only a piece of rough grazing land, part of the city's Town Moor. And since those Victorian years the ground has been steadily developed and redeveloped, although during the period, many controversial and intriguing moments have taken place as the club battled with their landlords and the planning authorities to make St James' Park a stadium to be proud of.

Previously home to Newcastle Rangers and Newcastle West End, United – then called East End – moved from their ground of Chillingham Road on the other side of the city to St James' Park in 1892. Substantial works took place around the turn of the century to turn the primitive arena near the Gallowgate into a ground fit for the club's new Division One status. Then in 1905 a major redevelopment of St James' Park began which transformed a 30,000-capacity stadium into a ground to match the very best, one that could hold up to 70,000 spectators.

But modernization in the following decades was carried out at a pace which frustrated everyone. By the time the Sixties arrived, St James' Park had become out of date, and the club lost the chance to stage 1966 World Cup finals matches because of a lack of redevelopment. The stadium had become recognized as one of the most uncomfortable and outdated grounds in the top flight.

Reconstruction

Development plans had been on the table for years. However, United's management not only had to contend with difficult planning issues – because of listed property adjacent to the stadium – but also, not being owners of the land, they had to negotiate any plans with Newcastle City Council as well as with the Freemen of the City who owned the Town Moor. And for decades the parties failed to agree on anything!

By the time the Taylor Report had been issued and accepted by all, Newcastle had managed to realize only one part of its new development plans. The East Stand was built in season 1972–73, but then financial restraints – and planning problems – stopped any further major work being carried out. The Magpies then

The Toon Army's home: St James' Park, as it neared completion in 1995. With a capacity of over 36,500, it is packed out for every game. A new, much bigger stadium is planned close by.

St James' Park as it was before 1970. The Leazes End is to the left, the Main Stand in the foreground.

ran into serious problems with the condition of the Main Stand, built in 1905. They went deep into debt to finance the reconstruction of the club's centre of activities, and also the Milburn Stand which opened in 1988.

As the Nineties dawned, Newcastle realized that to be able to complete the majority of the comprehensive redevelopment required, they needed a miracle – both on and off the field. That miracle arrived in the shape of Sir John Hall, who concluded a much-publicized takeover of the club. From then on, everything in the fortunes of Newcastle United changed: and the crucial issue of developing St James' Park into a stadium fit for the 21st century was high on Sir John's agenda.

With his financial backing and experience in property development, a completely new proposal was submitted for approval and a quick agreement was reached. The politics of confrontation of the past was forgotten and work started almost immediately to completely transform St James' Park, at a cost of almost £25 million. United would very quickly boast a ground to rival any in Britain.

Firstly the Leazes End stand – renamed the Sir John Hall Stand – was erected. It was opened for United's debut in the Premiership in 1993. Substantial alterations to the Milburn Stand were carried out, a new pitch and drainage system installed and new floodlighting, as well as the construction of the Gallowgate End structure, the Exhibition Stand. The corner infills were completed and the St James' Park bowl was complete, with impressive corporate and hospitality facilities which were the envy of other clubs.

With a capacity of more than 36,000 (presently 36,834) the stadium was ready in 1995, a showpiece well fitted to be a venue for the Euro '96 European Championships.

The Future

Newcastle United had one major problem still to be resolved. The capacity of the newly-redeveloped St James Park was only a little over 36,500. And due to restrictions in space and the engineering complexity of increasing the size of the Milburn Stand, United could not easily boost the capacity to a level which was needed. Newcastle had adopted a largely season-ticket-only policy from the day they entered the Premiership, but with the Magpies' huge following, and a growing demand for tickets, it became essential to allow more spectators into the ground.

However, to get regular attendances of between 40,000 and 50,000 at St James' Park, increased capacity was needed. Late in 1996 it was announced that the club was planning a new, much bigger stadium behind the present ground on Castle Leazes Moor. Plans were submitted for a £65 million development which would give United a 55,000-capacity, state-of-the-art ground to rival anything in the world. The plans included the remodelling of the present St James' Park stadium into a multi-purpose indoor leisure and sports centre, as well as a training complex for the club. Both facilities would be housed in a massive 55-acre complex integrated with new and refurbished parkland.

Newcastle supporters were excited at the prospect. The new plan averted the danger of United having to move from their traditional home near the city centre. As soon as permissions have been received, work will start on the Greater St James' Park.

St James' Park Factfile

LEAGUE AND CUP MATCHES

Top Attendance:
  68,386, vs Chelsea, Division One, 1930–31

Best Average Attendance:
  56,299, for season 1947–48

Record Gate Receipts:
  £744,544, vs Monaco, UEFA Cup, 1996–97

THE PREMIERSHIP YEARS

Average Home Attendances

1993–94	PL: 33,793	PL & Cup: 33,467
1994–95	PL: 34,692	PL & Cup: 33,935
1995–96	PL: 36,505	PL & Cup: 36,499
1996–97	PL: 36,467	PL & Cup: 36,067

The entrance to a field of noise! This is a player's view as he walks up the St James' Park tunnel and onto the pitch. As soon as the players appear, a cauldron of passionate support comes to the boil.

The Toon Army

It is doubtful that a more celebrated set of fans can be found in the country. Newcastle supporters have always been recognized as loyal and hugely passionate, as well as humorous and boisterous too. Football is born into families in the North-East, part of their heritage; and on Tyneside that means being born with black-and-white blood.

Football – and Newcastle United – is in many ways a way of life for thousands and thousands of Geordies. Their whole life revolves around the Magpies. And even if most of the population of Tyneside do not get to St James' Park, the majority still take an interest. Mothers, sisters, grandmothers all know about the club; their stars; the ups and downs; if they have won or if they have lost. Everyone wants United to succeed. Newcastle United is the flagship for the region and the population recognizes that and gives the club

unparalleled support both at home and away.

Even when things have not gone well – and there have been many tearful moments during the last 30 years – the fans have followed the club through thick and thin. They may have criticized the management – and noisily and persistently too – but always with the intention of making the Magpies the best in the country.

The Toon Army is almost legendary. Historically, the St James' Park crowd was well known for its vocal backing – worth a goal start to United, many opponents claimed. The atmosphere created at the stadium from the Leazes End, the Popular Terrace and the Gallowgate End was something quite special. And even now, with an all-seated stadium, the cauldron of noise that can be created for big matches cannot be equalled anywhere else.

With characters and personalities at every turn, the Toon Army are proud to tell everyone, wherever they are, that they belong to Newcastle and to Newcastle United. They wear the black-and-white shirt with immense pride, and any visitor to Tyneside will be astonished to see just how many people, both young and old, wear club colours for everyday use – never mind on match day.

Celebrity Fans

Chelsea are not the only club to have a row of high-profile supporters of the likes of John Major, Tony Banks, David Mellor and Sebastian Coe. Newcastle United can boast probably the most popular man in the country in Prime Minister Tony Blair as a supporter of their cause. Mr Blair, whose Sedgefield consituency is in County Durham, backed the club in his younger days, supporting the Magpies in the early Sixties and later, when players such as Malcolm "Supermac" Macdonald, Terry Hibbitt and Tony Green entertained the crowd. Jackie Milburn was a hero figure to him as a child, and Jimmy Smith was the Prime Minister's particular favourite in a black-and-white shirt. Even now, Tony Blair looks for United's result first.

Another dignitary to be a firm United fan is Cardinal Basil Hume, Archbishop of Westminster and head of the Roman Catholic Church in England and Wales. Brought up in Newcastle, Cardinal Hume has followed the Magpies since 1932 and was a fervent supporter in his younger days, watching United during the postwar period as well as following Gateshead

Left: The Toon Army's giant banner which travels to all of Newcastle's away games.
Below: Tony Blair, soon to become Prime Minister, displays a Newcastle shirt in company with then manager Kevin Keegan at Brighton in 1995.

during their Football League days. Now, from his Westminster home, Cardinal Hume constantly follows United's progress.

"Once a Geordie, always a Geordie" is a well-used expression. And being born in the Tyneside soccer hotbed means that even if you leave the area you still have a strong affinity with it – and with Newcastle United. Many personalities from television, film or music have retained their support for the club. *Auf Wiedersehen Pet's* Dennis, Oz and Neville – Tim Healy, Kevin Whatley and Jimmy Nail – have all developed even more successful careers since the days of that TV hit. Tim Healy, star of many programmes, has supported the club since he was a kid. Jimmy Nail is another fan. In fact, his family has a strong link with the club's success: a relation, Peter Mooney, actually played in Newcastle's 1924 FA Cup-winning side!

Robson Green is another United die-hard. The star of *Soldier Soldier*, and a host of subsequent screen hits, has watched the Magpies since his youth and was brought up yelling the praises of United's Seventies stars. A season-ticketholder in the Exhibition Stand along with his father, Robson delights in the spectacle of the match at St James' Park. He loves the whole day,

the preparation, the banter, the action, the noise – and the result and aftermath.

One star of stage and screen from a different era to give the Geordies his devotion is Norman Wisdom, loved by a different generation from Robson Green. The comedian and actor's love-affair with United started more than 40 years ago when he was in the Army. While he supports several clubs, he has always noted that there is something special about Newcastle United.

There are many other famous faces among the Magpies' support. Brian Johnson of rock band AC–DC is one; teen heart-throbs Ant and Dec, Sting and Brian Ferry; writer Ian La Frenais – who co-wrote *The Likely Lads* as well as many other classic television programmes such as *Porridge* and *Auf Wiedersehen Pet*. Athlete Brendan Foster is a passionate Newcastle supporter, as is racing tipster John McCririck who, even as a Londoner, is hooked on the Magpies.

The North-East Derbies

A derby clash in Liverpool, Manchester or Glasgow may have a more famous ring to it, but in the north-east corner of England a meeting between Newcastle United and Sunderland or Middlesbrough is as passionate as any other local fixture in the rest of the country. The Tyne–Wear clash is eagerly awaited in the North-East. For nearly 75 years it ranked as one of the top three or four matches of any season in the whole country.

Tyne vs Wear

The North-East's biggest communities lie barely nine miles apart, in a vast urban sprawl of nearly two million people – a population born with football in their blood. For much of football's history Newcastle and Sunderland were major forces in the game. An intense rivalry exists and Newcastle supporters, as representatives of the region's capital, consider United the more prestigious and enterprizing club in every way.

Rival skippers McCracken (right) and Thomson toss a coin before the start of a Tyne–Wear derby.

The rivalry started in Victorian times, when United's pioneer clubs Newcastle East End and West End first took on the men from the Wear – a club then in a much more advanced stage of development than their Tyneside rivals. The first recorded match was in 1883, Sunderland winning 3–0, but Newcastle West End gained quick revenge by knocking Sunderland out of the FA Cup.

By the time East End and West End had developed into Newcastle United and Football League status had been achieved in 1893, Sunderland were well on their way to becoming what was known as "The Team of All the Talent". They were champions for three years in that period; yet in the very first Football League clash during 1898 on Wearside, United won 3–2!

However, during those early years Sunderland's

superiority counted, and they claimed the lion's share of the results – until United embarked on their own period of mastery. There was an infamous riot on Good Friday, 1901, that saw the game abandoned before a ball was kicked, because a 70,000-strong crowd had packed into United's then much smaller St James' Park – a stadium that could only accommodate half that number.

United's first win at St James' Park came in 1902–03 and, in the process, they deprived Sunderland of the League title: then the Magpies started a period of dominance in the game and the tables were turned – except for one fateful day in 1908 when Sunderland scored nine goals to cause a sensation. United were on home soil – and were to become League Champions that season!

St James' Park was redeveloped and crowds of more than 60,000 were the norm for every fixture. Roker Park, too, had been enlarged and a similarly vast audience watched every derby encounter until modern times, when restrictions reduced the attendances dramatically.

The years between the wars saw the two rival camps evenly matched. United held the sway in the Twenties, Sunderland in the Thirties. In the 1920–21 season Newcastle gained a measure of revenge for that 1908 humiliation by winning 6–1 at St James' Park and 2–0 at Roker Park. They also got the better of their red-and-white rivals by winning a title chase with Sunderland and Huddersfield in 1927. The last Tyne vs. Wear battle at St James' Park before the Second World War took place in 1933–34. With United's impending relegation hanging over Tyneside Sunderland almost claimed both points, but an inspired United display and goals from England player Sammy Weaver gave the Magpies a valuable win. Newcastle were relegated, though, and derby games – apart from wartime encounters – were put on hold for almost 15 years.

The heyday of Newcastle and Sunderland rivalry came during the decade after the Second World War. United gained promotion quickly and joined Sunderland as one of the powers in the first division. Famous players graced the field: Shackleton, Milburn, Ford, Mitchell – the list was endless. In March 1950 a record crowd of 68,004 witnessed a 2–2 draw at Roker Park. Newcastle just had the edge in this fascinating

period: in the 1955–56 season they won 6–1 on Wearside and within 24 hours had won again on Tyneside, by 3–1, in a Christmas double-header. Yet that season typified the unpredictablity of any derby match, as Sunderland took victory later in the season in an epic FA Cup sixth-round meeting.

Relegation for the Red-and-Whites put a stop to the

Premiership derby action. Keith Gillespie (left) gets the better of Sunderland's Darius Kubicki.

deadly rivalry on the pitch. However, United's decline quickly followed, and in 1961 matches resumed, but for the first time in Division Two. Despite the lower grade of football, gates of 50,000 and more saw the Tyne battle it out with the Wear. There was one infamous occasion, however, when a hoax circulated throughout the region that a game had been postponed and it resulted in only 27,000 turning up for the match!

Results remained very even, and have done so until the last decade, since when Newcastle have held the advantage. Sunderland won a two-legged promotion play-off in 1990, but since then the Wearsiders have not defeated the Tynesiders. In the Premiership only two games have been played: Newcastle won 2–1 at Roker Park and drew 1–1 at St James' Park in 1996–97.

RECORD AGAINST SUNDERLAND

League and Cup fixtures

P	W	D	L	F	A
127	45	41	41	190	193

International stars Philippe Albert and Fabrizio Ravanelli tussle for possession at the Riverside Stadium.

Tyne vs Tees

While Newcastle's rivalry with the men from Teesside is still highly competitive, the passion and intensity of the derby encounter between United and Middlesbrough is not on the same level as that with Wearside. However, the Magpies have met the men from Middlesbrough in more than 100 games, and many have been thrilling and dramatic.

Newcastle's pioneers also met Boro on several occasions during the development of football in the North-East, but the first senior match took place in the 1892–93 FA Cup competition when Middlesbrough visited Tyneside. It proved a controversial start to the derby rivalry: Boro won 3–2, but after the game a huge row erupted when Newcastle's players were accused of not trying, and a bribery scandal erupted. An official inquiry followed – and it was concluded that bribery (of sorts) did in fact take place!

Football League action began in the 1902–03 season when Middlesbrough were elevated to Division One. Contests even themselves out over the decades, as is the case with matches against Sunderland. Newcastle just have the edge in victories – as they do also with Sunderland – but nothing can be taken for granted when Tyne squares up to Tees. Indeed Boro held the upper hand until they met in Premier League action.

In 1906–07 the Magpies scored four goals without reply on Tyneside and then went 40 miles down the coast to win 3–0 and record their best double in a year in which they won the title. Middlesbrough's best sequence of results in any season was a 5–0 victory at St James' Park during the 1930–31 season and a 3–1 success in the match at Ayresome Park.

In the Premiership, United and Middlesbrough have met over two campaigns. In 1995–96 Newcastle took all six points with a 1–0 home victory and a 2–1 win at Middlesbrough's new home, the Riverside Stadium. During 1996–97 the Magpies also won both games: 3–1 at St James' Park and 1–0 on Teesside.

RECORD AGAINST MIDDLESBROUGH

League and Cup fixtures

P	W	D	L	F	A
101	39	26	36	143	130

SUNDERLAND 1 (0)
NEWCASTLE UNITED 6 (4)
Football League Division 1
26 December 1955
Venue: Roker Park
Attendance: 55,723
Sunderland: Fraser, Hedley, McDonald, Anderson, Daniel, Aitken, Shackleton, Fleming, Purdon, Chisholm, Elliott.
Goal: Fleming (48)
United: Simpson, Batty, McMichael, Scoular, Paterson, Casey, Milburn, Davies, Keeble, Curry, Mitchell.
Goals: Keeble (2, 28), Milburn (12, 67), Curry (18, 81).

On Boxing Day 1955, Newcastle United gave their great rivals from Wearside their biggest hiding in the famous history of Tyne–Wear contests. In a season which saw both sides suffering from a similar lack of consistency, United were the side to raise their game in a white-hot atmosphere at a packed Roker Park.

They got off to a fabulous start. Within two minutes Newcastle were ahead when centre-forward Vic Keeble rocketed a header into the Sunderland net following a Casey free-kick. Newcastle's forward line was a menace to the home side and they could not stop the Black-and-Whites going 2–0 in front when Jackie Milburn whipped home a left-foot shot. With 18 minutes on the referee's watch Newcastle were 3–0 up as Bobby Mitchell passed to Bill Curry who scored from close in. And before half-time Keeble was on the mark again: his aerial presence was a constant problem to Sunderland's defenders and he rose high to head a Milburn corner into the net.

The Red-and-Whites were shell-shocked, and the second period saw Sunderland fare little better. They were totally outclassed, even though United did let the home side in for one chance, and Fleming pulled a goal back. Newcastle, though, soon increased their lead yet again.

Reg Davies found Jackie Milburn with a lovely lob, and "Wor Jackie" did the rest, flicking the ball past Fraser in the Roker goal. Then Mitchell crossed for young Bill Curry to grab his second goal and put United further ahead with a 6–1 advantage.

United were toying with their great rivals, and the only disappointment for Magpie fans was that they never went for the magic figure of nine goals – the number Sunderland netted against United back in 1908. United's fans did get another victory against the enemy to shout about, though – only 24 hours later at St James' Park.

MIDDLESBROUGH 0 (0)
NEWCASTLE UNITED 2 (2)
Football League Division 2
26 December 1964
Venue: Ayresome Park
Attendance: 38,184
Middlesbrough: Connachan, Ratcliffe, Jones, Townsend, Nurse, Orritt, Kaye, Gibson, Irvine, Masson, Braithwaite.
United: Marshall, Craig, Clark, Anderson, McGrath, Iley, Hockey, Hilley, McGarry, Penman, Suddick.
Goals: Hilley (20), Nurse (o.g., 27)

This was to prove a most important victory for Newcastle United. It was a crucial season for the club, the Magpies were top of Division Two and aiming to get promoted and follow Sunderland into Division One. With a number of clubs putting pressure on United at the top of the table, two points were vital for the Magpies.

Middlesbrough had some fine players within their ranks, among them Ian Gibson, Arthur Kaye, Mel Nurse, 18-year-old Don Masson and Bobby Braithwaite. Boro's famous manager Raich Carter tried to upset the St James' Park camp with some media swipes, but Newcastle let their football answer Carter's uncalled-for criticism.

United were fired up as a result of the attacks, and went into the lead after 20 minutes, when Dave Hilley latched on to a loose ball after goalkeeper Connachan had misjudged a Ron McGarry cross.

The game was all but over seven minutes later, and it was another scrappy goal that gave United their 2–0 advantage. Middlesbrough's centre-half Nurse attempted to control a long Stan Anderson free kick, then pass it back to his 'keeper – but the Welsh international defender only succeeded in firing the ball into his own net!

Comebacks are commonplace in football, but when Middlesbrough lost Orritt with an injury early in the second half a 10-man fightback became impossible – especially against United's mean rearguard.

In the festive holiday-period return match, two days later on Tyneside, Newcastle again came out on top. Scotsman Dave Hilley was once more on the mark, scoring twice to send a crowd of nearly 55,000 home delighted.

It was to prove an important double for the Magpies, because the four points secured at the expense of Boro enabled Newcastle to finish the season as champions of Division Two.

NEWCASTLE UNITED 2 (0)
MIDDLESBROUGH 1 (1)
Football League Division 1
1 February 1975
Venue: St James' Park
Attendance: 42,514
United: McFaul, Nattrass, Kennedy, Smith, Keeley, Howard, Barrowclough, Nulty, Macdonald, Burns, Craig. Sub: Bruce.
Goals: Macdonald (47), Burns (67).
Middlesbrough: Platt, Craggs, Spraggon, Souness, Boam, Maddren, Murdoch, Mills, Hickton, Foggon (Willey), Armstrong.
Goal: Hickton (7)

Newcastle twice needed to pick themselves off the floor for this contest against the men from Teesside. The Magpies had just been humiliatingly knocked out of the FA Cup by lowly Walsall and the team – and boss Joe Harvey in particular – had come in for much abuse in the days before this derby encounter. It took just seven minutes for United to find themselves a goal down to a Middlesbrough side, managed by Jack Charlton, which was riding high in Division One.

With players such as Graeme Souness, David Mills and Bobby Murdoch pulling the strings for Boro, as well as fielding ex-Magpies John Craggs and Alan Foggon, the visitors went ahead when John Hickton hit a beauty past Newcastle keeper Willie McFaul.

United struggled to get control of the game, with Souness showing the ability that was to make him such a big star with Liverpool. But the home side came out for the second half a different team, and produced a spirited display that transformed the game.

After only two minutes of the second half, United got back on level terms. Malcolm Macdonald sprinted into the Middlesbrough penalty area and, from an acute angle, "Supermac" struck a superb left-foot shot past Jim Platt.

The contest had now changed: all United had needed was that equalizing goal. The previously angry and frustrated crowd now yelled in support and the Magpies set about their local rivals with a period of sustained pressure. Tommy Craig and Jimmy Smith took command of midfield from Souness and the game swayed Newcastle's way.

The winner came from Micky Burns in the 67th minute. He picked up the ball on the left touchline, cut inside to enter the penalty area and then hit a great drive past Platt. The lead could have been added to as Burns, Craig and Stewart Barrowclough all went close to scoring for the Magpies.

NEWCASTLE UNITED 3 (1)
SUNDERLAND 1 (0)
Football League Division 1
1 January 1985
Venue: St James' Park
Attendance: 36,529
United: Carr, Brown, Saunders, Heard, Anderson, Clarke, Megson, Wharton, Baird, Beardsley, McDonald. Sub: Carney.
Goals: Beardsley (15, 48, 80).
Sunderland: Turner, Venison, Pickering, Daniel, Bennett, Berry, Gayle, Hodgson, West, Procter, Walker. Sub: Cooke.
Goal: West (71)

The New Year's Day meeting with Sunderland in the 1984–85 season was to be Peter Beardsley's day. Only a handful of players from either team have scored a derby hat-trick, and during the 90 minutes of action at St James' Park, Beardsley was in scintillating form, destroying the visitors with three well-taken goals.

Both clubs were struggling at the wrong end of Division One, but they served up a holiday treat – and, at times, an explosive clash. On a wet surface, United went in front after 15 minutes when Beardsley crashed in the first of his three efforts. A left-wing corner was knocked out to him on the edge of the box, and his low drive flashed past Chris Turner into the Reds' net.

Half-time came with the scoreline still 1–0, but the second period exploded into action almost immediately. Howard Gayle committed a bad foul on United full-back Wes Saunders in the penalty area: a clear penalty, but Gayle disagreed, argued with the referee and was sent to the dressing-room. Beardsley sent Turner the wrong way with a perfect spot-kick.

Ten minutes later there was a near carbon-copy of the previous incident. This time Kenny Wharton jinked his way into the box and it was Peter Daniel who sent him tumbling for another penalty. This time, however, Beardsley's kick was well saved by Turner.

The match became even more tense and furious. Tackles were becoming fiercer and more reckless. Sunderland pulled a goal back when Colin West surprised everybody with a lovely chip, but Beardsley hit back, moving into the penalty area to fire home his and Newcastle's third.

That, however, was not the end of the action. There was still time for Gary Bennett also to be sent off after another foul on Saunders. It was a rip-roaring derby: four goals, two penalties, two sendings-off and six bookings – and of course an exquisite Peter Beardsley hat-trick.

The Great Premiership Derbies

NEWCASTLE UNITED 1 (0)
MIDDLESBROUGH 0 (0)

FA Premiership

Wednesday 30 August 1995

Venue: St James' Park

Attendance: 36,483.

United: Hislop, Barton, Beresford, Peacock, Howey, Lee, Beardsley, Ferdinand, Clark, Ginola, Gillespie. Subs not used: Fox, Srnicek, Hottiger.

Goal: Ferdinand (72).

Middlesbrough: Miller, Cox, Morris, Vickers, Pearson, Whyte, Barmby, Pollock, Fjortoft, Mustoe, Hignett (Moreno). Subs not used: Whelan, Kavanagh.

When Newcastle met Bryan Robson's newly-promoted Middlesbrough in the opening weeks of the 1995–96 Premier League season, Newcastle were red-hot. The addition of Les Ferdinand and David Ginola to United's forward line had an immediate effect. Their record read: played three, won three, and a fourth victory would put the Magpies on top of the table.

A packed St James' Park crowd saw United play to their attacking strengths and Frenchman David Ginola, in particular, displayed his flamboyant skills to the full. Ginola, nicknamed *Le Magnifique* – "the magnificent one" – in his home country, quickly became a favourite of the Toon Army. And Middlesbrough couldn't handle his twists and turns, his pace along the left flank, not to mention moments of sheer brilliance on the ball. One magnificent jink and drag back of the ball deep in defence sent Boro players sprawling and was worth the price of admission alone.

With the visitors packing their defence, Newcastle dominated the game. They should have won the match by more than the single goal that settled the fixture. Newcastle went close through Ferdinand, Keith Gillespie, Ginola and Robert Lee, while visiting goalkeeper Alan

Les Ferdinand has just scored from David Ginola's cross and happy teammates congratulate the striker.

Miller pulled off some tremendous saves. But Newcastle's pressure eventually paid off midway through the second half – and it was a quality strike.

All evening Ginola had displayed a level of skill on the ball rarely seen in this country, and the Frenchman opened up Boro's rearguard with a dazzling run close to the touchline. He swivelled and curled in a tantalizing cross. In stormed Les Ferdinand to power a stunning header into the Middlesbrough net for a picture goal.

Middlesbrough now had to attack to save the game, and a more open contest developed. Newcastle found more space and almost hit them on the break on more than one occasion. Gillespie and Warren Barton caused havoc, as did Ginola, who set up Ferdinand with another scintillating run and cross.

However, Boro almost claimed an equalizer in the dying minutes when Jamie Pollock went down in the penalty area after a challenge from Darren Peacock. Despite vociferous appeals, the referee refused Boro's claim for a penalty and Newcastle secured the points.

SUNDERLAND 1 (1)
NEWCASTLE UNITED 2 (0)

FA Premiership
Wednesday 4 September 1996
Venue: Roker Park
Attendance: 22,037
Sunderland: Coton, Kubicki, Scott, Bracewell, Ball, Melville, Gray, Ord, Stewart (Russell), Agnew (Rae), Quinn. Subs not used: Preece, Bridges Aiston.
Goal: Scott (20).

United: Srnicek, Watson, Elliott, Batty, Howey, Peacock, Lee, Beardsley, Shearer, Ferdinand (Clark), Ginola. Subs not used: Hislop, Asprilla, Albert, Gillespie.
Goals: Beardsley (52), Ferdinand (63).

The derby fixture with Sunderland at the start of the 1996–97 season was memorable for several reasons. It was the first match between the two rivals for four years; it was the last at Roker Park before the Reds moved to the Stadium of Light; and it was also the first to be without any visiting supporters, United's fans being controversially banned in an all-ticket clash.

As a result, the Roker Park atmosphere was unique. Newcastle had no support, apart from their visiting officials and directors, and the mood was distinctly hostile. For the opening 45 minutes, the Magpies' players found the abnormal conditions very difficult. The Wearsiders stormed forward, giving United a torrid time, and it was no surprise when they opened the scoring. In the 19th minute, Robbie Elliott felled Steve Agnew in the penalty area, and Martin Scott stepped up to drive the ball past Srnicek from the spot.

For the rest of the first half, the Wearsiders laid siege on United's goal, but they could not score a second to give them a cushion. The half-time break gave the Magpies' boss Kevin Keegan the chance to make some changes and inspire his team to a second-half revival.

Newcastle needed to dig deep to turn the game around. After the interval they did exactly that, and the second period was as good for United as the first half had been bad. Peter Beardsley and David Ginola began to make an impression and Newcastle controlled the midfield through David Batty and Rob Lee. Beardsley scored the equalizer with a rare header after Les Ferdinand had run down the right wing to cross.

Ferdinand was proving the big danger man and he netted the winner after 63 minutes. Ginola's precision corner-kick found the big striker, who rose to meet the ball with power. Goalkeeper Tony Coton could only watch as it flashed into the net.

The winner was met with silence at Roker, but a few miles away, at the Newcastle Arena, thousands of United fans, watching on a giant screen, were yelling with joy. It was indeed a unique derby confrontation.

David Batty's run is halted by a challenge from Sunderland's Paul Bracewell in the derby match at Roker Park. It was the final Wear–Tyne match to be played at the famous venue before the Wearsiders moved to their new Stadium of Light.

Chapter 12

The Records

Year-by-year statistics

Season 1993–94

COCA-COLA CUP					
Date	**Team**	**Venue**	**Att**	**Score**	**Scorers**
2nd Round					
23 Sept	Notts County	H	25,687	4–1	Cole (3), Bracewell
5 Oct	Notts County	A	6,068	7–1	Cole (3), Allen (2), Lee, Beardsley
3rd Round					
27 Oct	Wimbledon	A	11,531	1–2	Sellars

FA CUP					
Date	**Team**	**Venue**	**Att**	**Score**	**Scorers**
3rd Round					
8 Jan	Coventry City	H	35,444	2–0	Cole, Beardsley
4th Round					
29 Jan	Luton Town	H	32,216	1–1	Beardsley
Replay					
9 Feb	Luton Town	A	12,503	0–2	

APPEARANCES & GOALSCORERS			
Name	**Apps**	**(Sub)**	**Goals**
Pavel Srnicek	22		
Barrry Venison	41	(1)	
John Beresford	40		
Paul Bracewell	36		2
Kevin Scott	21		
Ruel Fox	14		2
Steve Howey	16	(1)	
Robert Lee	47		8
Peter Beardsley	41		24
Andy Cole	45		41
Lee Clark	34		2
Scott Sellars	33	(2)	4
Mark Robinson	13	(4)	
Tommy Wright	2	(1)	
Alex Mathie	1	(16)	3
Brian Kilcline	2	(2)	
Darren Peacock	9		
Liam O'Brien	4	(2)	
Nicky Papavasiliou	7		
Steve Watson	34	(4)	2
Alan Neilson	10	(4)	
Malcolm Allen	12		7
Chris Holland	2	(1)	
Matty Appleby	1		
Robbie Elliott	15	(2)	
Mike Hooper	24		
Mike Jeffrey	2		
Own Goals			2

Date	Team	Venue	Att	Score	Scorers
14 Aug	Tottenham Hotspur	H	35,216	0–1	
18 Aug	Coventry City	A	15,760	1–2	own goal
21 Aug	Manchester United	A	41,829	1–1	Cole
25 Aug	Everton	H	34,833	1–0	Allen
29 Aug	Blackburn Rovers	H	34,272	1–1	Cole
31 Aug	Ipswich Town	A	19,102	1–1	Cole
13 Sept	Sheffield Wednesday	H	33,890	4–2	Cole (2), Allen, Mathie
18 Sept	Swindon Town	A	15,015	2–2	Clark, Allen
25 Sept	West Ham United	H	34,366	2–0	Cole (2)
2 Oct	Aston Villa	A	37,336	2–0	Cole, Allen
16 Oct	Queens Park Rangers	H	33,926	1–2	Allen
24 Oct	Southampton	A	13,804	1–2	Cole
30 Oct	Wimbledon	H	33,392	4–0	Beardsley (3), Cole
8 Nov	Oldham Athletic	A	13,821	3–1	Beardsley, Cole (2)
21 Nov	Liverpool	H	36,374	3–0	Cole (3)
24 Nov	Sheffield United	H	35,101	4–0	Beardsley (2), Cole, own goal
27 Nov	Arsenal	A	36,091	1–2	Beardsley
4 Dec	Tottenham Hotspur	A	30,780	2–1	Beardsley (2)
11 Dec	Manchester United	H	36,388	1–1	Cole
18 Dec	Everton	A	25,189	2–0	Beardsley, Cole
22 Dec	Leeds United	H	36,388	1–1	Cole
28 Dec	Chelsea	A	22,133	0–1	
1 Jan	Manchester City	H	35,658	2–0	Cole (2)
4 Jan	Norwich City	A	19,564	2–1	Beardsley, Cole
16 Jan	Queens Park Rangers	A	15,774	2–1	Beardsley, Clark
22 Jan	Southampton	H	32,129	1–2	Cole
12 Feb	Wimbledon	A	13,358	2–4	Beardsley (2)
19 Feb	Blackburn Rovers	A	21,269	0–1	
23 Feb	Coventry City	H	32,216	4–0	Cole (3), Mathie
5 Mar	Sheffield Wednesday	A	33,224	1–0	Cole
12 Mar	Swindon Town	H	32,216	7–1	Watson (2), Lee (2), Beardsley (2), Fox
19 Mar	West Ham United	A	23,132	4–2	Lee (2), Cole, Mathie
23 Mar	Ipswich Town	H	32,216	2–0	Cole, Sellars
29 Mar	Norwich City	H	32,216	3–0	Lee, Beardsley, Cole
1 Apr	Leeds United	A	40,005	1–1	Cole
4 Apr	Chelsea	H	32,216	0–0	
9 Apr	Manchester City	A	33,774	1–2	Sellars
16 Apr	Liverpool	A	44,601	2–0	Lee, Cole
23 Apr	Oldham Athletic	H	32,216	3–2	Lee, Beardsley, Fox
27 Apr	Aston Villa	H	32,216	5–1	Bracewell, Beardsley (2), Cole, Sellars
30 Apr	Sheffield United	A	29,013	0–2	
7 May	Arsenal	H	32,216	2–0	Beardsley, Cole

Final League Position: Third

Season 1994–95

FA PREMIER LEAGUE					
Date	Team	Venue	Att	Score	Scorers
21 Aug	Leicester City	A	20,048	3–1	Beardsley, Cole, Elliott
24 Aug	Coventry City	H	34,163	4–0	Lee (2), Cole, Watson
27 Aug	Southampton	H	34,182	5–1	Lee, Cole (2), Watson (2)
31 Aug	West Ham United	A	17,375	3–1	Lee, Mathie, own goal
10 Sept	Chelsea	H	34,435	4–2	Fox, Lee, Cole (2)
18 Sept	Arsenal	A	36,819	3–2	Fox, Beardsley (2)
24 Sept	Liverpool	H	34,435	1–1	Lee
1 Oct	Aston Villa	A	29,960	2–0	Lee, Cole
9 Oct	Blackburn Rovers	H	34,344	1–1	own goal
15 Oct	Crystal Palace	A	17,739	1–0	Beardsley
22 Oct	Sheffield Wednesday	H	34,408	2–1	Cole, Watson
29 Oct	Manchester United	A	43,795	0–2	
5 Nov	Queens Park Rangers	H	34,278	2–1	Beardsley, Kitson
7 Nov	Nottingham Forest	A	22,102	0–0	
19 Nov	Wimbledon	A	14,203	2–3	Beardsley, Kitson
26 Nov	Ipswich Town	H	34,459	1–1	Cole
3 Dec	Tottenham Hotspur	A	28,002	2–4	Fox (2)
10 Dec	Leicester City	H	34,400	3–1	Howey, Albert (2)
17 Dec	Coventry City	A	17,237	0–0	
26 Dec	Leeds United	A	39,337	0–0	
31 Dec	Norwich City	A	21,172	1–2	Fox
2 Jan	Manchester City	H	34,437	0–0	
15 Jan	Manchester United	H	34,471	1–1	Kitson
21 Jan	Sheffield Wednesday	A	31,215	0–0	
25 Jan	Wimbledon	H	34,374	2–1	Fox, Kitson
1 Feb	Everton	H	34,465	2–0	Fox, Beardsley
4 Feb	Queens Park Rangers	A	16,576	0–3	
11 Feb	Nottingham Forest	H	34,471	2–1	Fox, Lee
25 Feb	Aston Villa	H	34,637	3–1	Venison, Beardsley (2)
28 Feb	Ipswich Town	A	18,639	2–0	Fox, Kitson
4 Mar	Liverpool	A	39,300	0–2	
8 Mar	West Ham United	H	34,595	2–0	Clark, Kitson
19 Mar	Arsenal	H	35,611	1–0	Beardsley
22 Mar	Southampton	A	14,666	1–3	Kitson
1 Apr	Chelsea	A	22,987	1–1	Hottiger
8 Apr	Norwich City	H	35,518	3–0	Beardsley (2), Kitson
14 Apr	Everton	A	34,628	0–2	
17 Apr	Leeds United	H	35,626	1–2	Elliott
29 Apr	Manchester City	A	27,389	0–0	
3 May	Tottenham Hotspur	H	35,603	3–3	Beardsley, Peacock, Gillespie
8 May	Blackburn Rovers	A	30,545	0–1	
14 May	Crystal Palace	H	35,626	3–2	Fox, Lee, Gillespie

Final League position: Sixth

COCA-COLA CUP

Date	Team	Venue	Att	Score	Scorers
2nd Round					
21 Sept	Barnsley	H	27,208	2–1	Cole, Fox
5 Oct	Barnsley	A	10,992	1–0	Cole
3rd Round					
26 Oct	Manchester U.	H	34,178	2–0	Kitson, Albert
4th Round					
30 Nov	Manchester C.	A	25,162	1–1	Jeffrey
Replay					
21 Dec	Manchester C.	H	31,056	0–2	

FA CUP

Date	Team	Venue	Att	Score	Scorers
3rd Round					
8 Jan	Blackburn R.	H	31,721	1–1	Lee
Replay					
18 Jan	Blackburn R.	A	22,658	2–1	Clark, Hottiger
4th Round					
28 Jan	Swansea City	H	34,372	3–0	Kitson (3)
5th Round					
19 Feb	Manchester C.	H	33,219	3–1	Gillespie (2), Beresford
Quarter-final					
12 Mar	Everton	A	35,203	0–1	

UEFA CUP

Date	Team	Venue	Att	Score	Scorers
1st Round					
13 Sept	Royal Antwerp	A	19,700	5–0	Lee (3), Sellars, Watson
27 Sept	Royal Antwerp	H	31,383	5–2	Cole (3), Beardsley, Lee
2nd Round					
18 Oct	Athletic Bilbao	H	32,440	3–2	Cole, Beardsley, Fox
1 Nov	Athletic Bilbao	A	47,000	0–1	

APPEARANCES & GOALSCORERS

Name	Apps	(Sub)	Goals
Pavel Srnicek	52		
Barrry Venison	36		1
John Beresford	46		1
Paul Bracewell	16	(4)	
Ruel Fox	51		12
Steve Howey	39	(1)	1
Robert Lee	44		14
Peter Beardsley	44		15
Andy Cole	27		15
Lee Clark	15	(12)	2
Scott Sellars	19		1
Marc Hottiger	51		2
Alex Mathie	4	(8)	1
Darren Peacock	48		1
Steve Guppy		(1)	
Keith Gillespie	18	(2)	4
Steve Watson	26	(9)	5
Alan Neilson	6	(1)	
Malcolm Allen		(1)	
Robbie Elliott	13	(5)	2
Philippe Albert	25		3
Paul Kitson	31	(3)	12
Mike Hooper	4	(2)	
Mike Jeffrey	1	(2)	1
Own Goals			2

Season 1995–96

FA PREMIER LEAGUE					
Date	**Team**	**Venue**	**Att**	**Score**	**Scorers**
19 Aug	Coventry City	H	36,485	3–0	Lee, Beardsley, Ferdinand
22 Aug	Bolton Wanderers	A	20,243	3–1	Lee, Ferdinand (2)
27 Aug	Sheffield Wednesday	A	24,815	2–0	Beardsley, Ginola
30 Aug	Middlesbrough	H	36,483	1–0	Ferdinand
9 Sept	Southampton	A	15,237	0–1	
16 Sept	Manchester City	H	36,501	3–1	Beardsley, Ferdinand (2)
24 Sept	Chelsea	H	36,225	2–0	Ferdinand (2)
1 Oct	Everton	A	33,080	3–1	Lee, Ferdinand, Kitson
14 Oct	Queens Park Rangers	A	18,254	3–2	Ferdinand, Gillespie (2)
21 Oct	Wimbledon	H	36,434	6–1	Clark, Howey, Ferdinand (3), Albert
29 Oct	Tottenham Hotspur	A	32,279	1–1	Ginola
4 Nov	Liverpool	H	36,547	2–1	Watson, Ferdinand
8 Nov	Blackburn Rovers	H	36,463	1–0	Lee
18 Nov	Aston Villa	A	39,167	1–1	Ferdinand
25 Nov	Leeds United	H	36,572	2–1	Lee, Beardsley
3 Dec	Wimbledon	A	18,002	3–3	Ferdinand (2), Gillespie
9 Dec	Chelsea	A	31,098	0–1	
16 Dec	Everton	H	36,557	1–0	Ferdinand
23 Dec	Nottingham Forest	H	36,531	3–1	Lee (2), Ginola
27 Dec	Manchester United	A	42,024	0–2	
2 Jan	Arsenal	H	36,530	2–0	Ferdinand, Ginola
14 Jan	Coventry City	A	20,547	1–0	Watson
20 Jan	Bolton Wanderers	H	36,543	2–1	Beardsley, Kitson
3 Feb	Sheffield Wednesday	H	36,567	2–0	Clark, Ferdinand
10 Feb	Middlesbrough	A	30,011	2–1	Ferdinand, Watson
21 Feb	West Ham United	A	23,843	0–2	
24 Feb	Manchester City	A	31,115	3–3	Albert (2), Asprilla
4 Mar	Manchester United	H	36,584	0–1	
18 Mar	West Ham United	H	36,331	3–0	Albert, Ferdinand, Asprilla
23 Mar	Arsenal	A	38,271	0–2	
3 Apr	Liverpool	A	40,702	3–4	Ferdinand, Asprilla, Ginola
6 Apr	Queens Park Rangers	H	36,583	2–1	Beardsley (2)
8 Apr	Blackburn Rovers	A	30,717	1–2	Batty
14 Apr	Aston Villa	H	36,510	1–0	Ferdinand
17 Apr	Southampton	H	36,554	1–0	Lee
29 Apr	Leeds United	A	38,862	1–0	Gillespie
2 May	Nottingham Forest	A	28,280	1–1	Beardsley
5 May	Tottenham Hotspur	H	36,589	1–1	Ferdinand

Final League position: Second

FA CUP

Date	Team	Venue	Att	Score	Scorers
3rd Round					
7 Jan	Chelsea	A	25,151	1–1	Ferdinand
Replay					
17 Jan	Chelsea	H	36,535	2–2 (Lost on pens 2–4)	Albert, Beardsley (pen)

COCA-COLA CUP

Date	Team	Venue	Att	Score	Scorers
2nd Round					
19 Sept	Bristol City	A	15,952	5–0	Peacock, Sellars, Ferdinand, Gillespie, Lee
4 Oct	Bristol City	H	36,357	3–1	Barton, Albert, Ferdinand
3rd Round					
25 Oct	Stoke City	A	23,000	4–0	Beardsley (2), Ferdinand, Peacock
4th Round					
29 Nov	Liverpool	A	40,077	1–0	Watson
Quarter-final					
10 Jan	Arsenal	A	37,857	0–2	

APPEARANCES & GOALSCORERS

Name	Apps	(Sub)	Goals
Pavel Srnicek	17	(2)	
Warren Barton	37	(1)	1
John Beresford	35	(1)	
Darren Peacock	40	(1)	2
Ruel Fox	3	(2)	
Steve Howey	33		1
Robert Lee	41		9
Peter Beardsley	40		11
Les Ferdinand	44		29
Lee Clark	26	(7)	2
Scott Sellars	4	(4)	1
Faustino Asprilla	11	(3)	3
Marc Hottiger	1	(2)	
David Ginola	40		5
Shaka Hislop	28		
Darren Huckerby		(2)	
Jimmy Crawford		(1)	
Keith Gillespie	30	(2)	5
Steve Watson	18	(11)	4
David Batty	11		1
Chris Holland		(1)	
Paul Brayson	1		
Robbie Elliott	8	(2)	
Philippe Albert	23	(5)	6
Paul Kitson	4	(5)	2

Season 1996–97

			FA PREMIER LEAGUE		
Date	**Team**	**Venue**	**Att**	**Score**	**Scorers**
17 Aug	Everton	A	40,117	0–2	
21 Aug	Wimbledon	H	36,385	2–0	Batty, Shearer
24 Aug	Sheffield Wednesday	H	36,452	1–2	Shearer
4 Sept	Sunderland	A	22,037	2–1	Ferdinand, Beardsley
7 Sept	Tottenham Hotspur	A	32,535	2–1	Ferdinand (2)
14 Sept	Blackburn Rovers	H	36,424	2–1	Ferdinand, Shearer
21 Sept	Leeds United	A	36,070	1–0	Shearer
30 Sept	Aston Villa	H	36,400	4–3	Ferdinand (2), Shearer, Howey
12 Oct	Derby County	A	18.092	1–0	Shearer
20 Oct	Manchester United	H	36,579	5–0	Albert, Ginola, Ferdinand, Shearer, Peacock
26 Oct	Leicester City	A	21,134	0–2	
3 Nov	Middlesbrough	H	36,577	3–1	Beardsley (2), Lee
16 Nov	West Ham United	H	36,552	1–1	Beardsley
23 Nov	Chelsea	A	28,401	1–1	Shearer
30 Nov	Arsenal	H	36,565	1–2	Shearer
9 Dec	Nottingham Forest	A	25,762	0–0	
17 Dec	Coventry City	A	21,538	1–2	Shearer
23 Dec	Liverpool	H	36,570	1–1	Shearer
26 Dec	Blackburn Rovers	A	30,398	0–1	
28 Dec	Tottenham Hotspur	H	36,308	7–1	Albert, Ferdinand (2), Shearer (2), Lee (2)
1 Jan	Leeds United	H	36,489	3–0	Ferdinand, Shearer (2)
11 Jan	Aston Villa	A	39,339	2–2	Clark, Shearer
18 Jan	Southampton	A	15,251	2–2	Clark, Ferdinand
29 Jan	Everton	H	36,143	4–1	Elliott, Ferdinand, Shearer, Lee
2 Feb	Leicester City	H	36,396	4–3	Elliott, Shearer (3)
22 Feb	Middlesbrough	A	30,063	1–0	Ferdinand
1 Mar	Southampton	H	36,446	0–1	
10 Mar	Liverpool	A	40,751	3–4	Gillespie, Asprilla, Barton
15 Mar	Coventry City	H	36,571	4–0	Elliott, Watson, Beardsley, Lee
23 Mar	Wimbledon	A	23,175	1–1	Asprilla
5 Apr	Sunderland	H	36,582	1–1	Shearer
13 Apr	Sheffield Wednesday	A	33,798	1–1	Elliott
16 Apr	Chelsea	H	36,320	3–1	Asprilla, Shearer (2)
19 Apr	Derby County	H	36,553	3–1	Elliott, Ferdinand, Shearer
3 May	Arsenal	A	38,179	1–0	Elliott
6 May	West Ham United	A	24,617	0–0	
8 May	Manchester United	A	55,236	0–0	
11 May	Nottingham Forest	H	36,554	5–0	Elliott, Asprilla, Ferdinand (2), Shearer

Final League position: Second

FA CUP

Date	Team	Venue	Att	Score	Scorers
3rd Round					
5 Jan	Charlton Athletic	A	14,980	1–1	Lee
3rd Round Replay					
15 Jan	Charlton Athletic	H	36,398	2–1	Clark, Shearer
4th Round					
26 Jan	Nottingham F.	H	36,434	1–2	Ferdinand

UEFA CUP

Date	Team	Venue	Att	Score	Scorers
1st Round					
10 Sept	Halmstad	H	28,124	4–0	Ferdinand, Asprilla, Albert, Beardsley
24 Sept	Halmstad	A	7,847	1–2	Ferdinand
2nd Round					
15 Oct	Ferencvaros	A	18,000	2–3	Ferdinand, Shearer
29 Oct	Ferencvaros	H	35,740	4–0	Asprilla (2), Ginola, Ferdinand
3rd Round					
19 Nov	Metz	A	23,000	1–1	Beardsley (pen)
3 Dec	Metz	H	35,641	2–0	Asprilla (2)
Quarter–Final					
4 Mar	Monaco	H	36,215	0–1	
18 Mar	Monaco	A	18,500	0–3	

COCA-COLA CUP

Date	Team	Venue	Att	Score	Scorers
3rd Round					
23 Oct	Oldham Ath.	H	36,314	1–0	Beardsley (pen)
4th Round					
27 Nov	Middlesbrough	A	29,831	1–3	Shearer

APPEARANCES & GOALSCORERS

Name	Apps	(Sub)	Goals
Pavel Srnicek	29		
Warren Barton	20	(7)	1
John Beresford	24	(2)	
Darren Peacock	48		1
Steve Howey	9		1
Robert Lee	43	(1)	6
Peter Beardsley	33	(3)	8
Alan Shearer	39		28
Les Ferdinand	37	(2)	21
Faustino Asprilla	25	(7)	9
David Ginola	30	(5)	2
Shaka Hislop	22		
Jimmy Crawford		(2)	
Keith Gillespie	31	(12)	1
Steve Watson	39	(6)	1
Lee Clark	14	(20)	3
David Batty	44		1
Robbie Elliott	36	(2)	7
Philippe Albert	38	(1)	3
Paul Kitson		(6)	

Miscellaneous Premiership Records

These statistics cover United's Premier League matches 1993–94 to 1996–97 inclusive. Appearances include those where a substitute came on.

Team Records

OVERALL RECORD						
P	**W**	**D**	**L**	**F**	**A**	**Pts**
160	86	37	37	288	165	295

Win ratio of 54%
Defeat ratio of 23%
Strike-rate ratio of 1.80 goals per game

HOME RECORD						
P	**W**	**D**	**L**	**F**	**A**	**Pts**
80	58	14	8	189	63	188

Win ratio of 73%
Defeat ratio of 10%
Strike-rate ratio of 2.36 goals per game

AWAY RECORD						
P	**W**	**D**	**L**	**F**	**A**	**Pts**
80	28	23	29	99	102	107

Win ratio of 35%
Defeat ratio of 36%
Strike-rate ratio of 1.24 goals per game

HIGHS AND LOWS

Biggest victories

7–1 v Swindon Town (H) 1993–94

7–1 v Tottenham Hotspur (H) 1996–97

Heaviest defeats

0–3 v Queens Park Rangers (A) 1994–95

Biggest away victory

4–2 v West Ham United 1993–94

(Also several 3–1 & 2–0 wins)

Heaviest home defeat

0–1 or 1–2 against several clubs

Most points

78 in season 1995–96 (position 2nd)

Fewest points

68 in season 1996–97 (position 2nd)

Most goals for

82 in season 1993–94

Fewest goals for

66 in season 1995–96

Most goals against

47 in season 1994–95

Fewest goals against

40 in season 1996–97

Most victories

24 in season 1995–96

Fewest wins

19 in season 1996–97

Fewest defeats

8 in season 1995–96 and 1996–97

Most defeats

11 in season 1993–94

Most draws

12 in season 1994–95

Fewest draws

6 in season 1995–96

SEQUENCES AND TOTALS

Unbeaten sequence at home

26 games; 1993–94 running into 1994–95

Most home wins in a season

17 in season 1995–96

Longest run without a home win in a season

3 games; 1996–97

Most home defeats in a season

3 games; 1993–94, 1996–97

Most away victories in a season

9 in season 1993–94

Most away defeats in a season

9 in season 1994–95

Longest unbeaten run

12 games; 1993–94 running into 1994–95

Longest run without a victory

7 games; 1996–97

Worst run of results

One win between 20 October and 28 December 1996

Most victories in a row

7 in season 1994–95 running into 1995–96, 7 in season 1996–97

Most home victories in a row

14 games; 1994–95 running into 1995–96

Most away victories in a row

5 games; 1994–95

Most defeats in a row

3 games; 1993–94

ATTENDANCES

Top home attendance

36,589 v Tottenham Hotspur 1995–96

Top away attendance

55,236 v Manchester United 1996–97

Individual Records

GOALSCORING

Best individual scoring in a season

34 goals by Andy Cole in 1993–94

Highest scorer (Premier League only)

Peter Beardsley 47 goals 1993–1997

Top scorers per season

1993–94 Andy Cole 34 goals
1994–95 Peter Beardsley 13 goals
1995–96 Les Ferdinand 25 goals
1996–97 Alan Shearer 25 goals

Top five aggregate goalscorers

1 Peter Beardsley 47 goals
2 Andy Cole 43 goals
3 Les Ferdinand 41 goals
4 Robert Lee 29 goals
5 Alan Shearer 25 goals

Most hat-tricks

2 by Andy Cole

APPEARANCES

Longest run of appearances

47 consecutive appearances by Robert Lee between 29 August 1993 and 9 October 1994

Top five aggregate appearances

1 Robert Lee 145 games
2 Peter Beardsley 129 games
3 John Beresford 119 games
4 Steve Watson 118 games
5 Darren Peacock 113 games

Index

Acknowledgements

The publishers would like to thank the following sources for their kind permission to reproduce the pictures in this book:

Allsport UK Ltd./Shaun Botterill, Clive Brunskill, Graham Chadwick, Chris Cole, Stu Forster, Clive Mason, Ben Radford, Mark Thompson, Anton Want; Allsport Historical Collection/Hulton Getty; Stewart Bonney (News) Agency; Colorsport; Empics/Laurence Griffiths, Tony Marshall, Steve Morton, Neal Simpson, Aubrey Washington; Hulton Getty; Mark Leech; North News and Pictures; PA News; Popperfoto/Russell Boyce, Reuters; Professional Sport; Sporting Pictures (UK) Ltd.

Every effort has been made to acknowledge correctly and contact the source and/copyright holder of each picture, and Carlton Books Limited apologises for any unintentional errors or omissions which will be corrected in future editions of this book.